AMERICA'S WILD HORSES

AMERICA'S WILD HORSES

The History of the Western Mustang

Steve Price

Skyhorse Publishing

Skyhorse Publishing books may be purchased in bulk at special discounts for sales promotion, corporate gifts, fund-raising, or educational purposes. Special editions can also be created to specifications. For details, contact the Special Sales Department, Skyhorse Publishing, 307 West 36th Street, 11th Floor, New York, New York 10018 or info@skyhorsepublishing.com

Skyhorse® and Skyhorse Publishing® are registered trademarks of Skyhorse Publishing Inc.®, a Delaware Corporation

www.skyhorsepublishing.com

10 9 8 7 6

Library of Congress Cataloging-in-Publication Data is available on file.

Cover design by Tom Lau
Cover photo credit: Steve Price

Print ISBN: 978-1-63450-393-8
Ebook ISBN: 978-1-63450-394-5

Printed in China

To Ann,
who loves riding the high country as much as I do

Contents

Foreword

I don't think it's a coincidence that the first truly authentic country song written by the Rolling Stones was titled "Wild Horses," or that when the Ford Motor Company was looking to launch a sports car it hoped would capture the spirit of a new generation in the mid-1960s, it chose to call the car "Mustang."

Such is the hold these magnificent animals have on our imagination. And what would the American West be without it?

It wouldn't.

When we think of disruptive technologies these days, we tend to think about the microchip, the personal computer, or the smartphone. But the horse in its day was just as transformative. By allowing mankind to move faster, carry more, plant more, and yes, make war more efficiently, it changed societies, in the process sweeping away the ways of the old. In this remarkable book, Steve Price chronicles the history of the horse, especially the one Americans know as the Western Mustang. Like many Americans, it has a complicated heritage, with strands from the steppes of the Ukraine, the shores of the Barbary Coast, the rugged terrain of Spain's Andalusia, and the swirling winds of the Arabian Desert. It's these strains that give the horse its unique characteristics, especially its intelligence and speed.

Though horses were present in North America early on, they died out, possibly being hunted to extinction by early humans. Only by crossing the frozen Bering Strait into Asia did they survive. The re-introduction of the animals by the Spanish conquistadors during the sixteenth century ultimately transformed the Native American culture of what was then known as the Great American Desert, turning some, particularly the Comanche, into superb horsemen. That strategic advantage was one reason the US government began a horse extermination program during the Indian Wars of the late nineteenth century. And sadly, Steve also chronicles how we nearly lost the remnants of these herds before committed horsemen and women decided to take a stand and alter the practice of wholesale slaughter for dog food.

Akin to the modern issue of multiple use by hunters, trail bikers, and hikers in national forests and parks, the wild horse competes with domestic cattle and sheep for a place to graze. And like modern game management, these wild horses must be managed or they would quickly out-graze the land. It's a complex issue involving government management and private property rights, a story that is still playing out today in many areas of the West.

As an editor at *Field & Stream*, I worked with Steve for many years. In those days, he was known mainly as a "bass guy," meaning he focused on the largemouth bass, often considered America's most popular gamefish. But as I got to know him, I realized he was a man of many interests. For example, he was also an astute observer of African wildlife, particularly lions and leopards, and after months of filming them, I believe he understood the big cats nearly as well as he understood the habits of the bass, as evidenced by his 2007 book, *Valley of the Big Cats*.

When he moved to Wyoming, we talked about heading up into the Wind River Mountains, where he lived, by horse to reach alpine trout streams. The trip never happened, but it was then, and later when he resettled to New Mexico, that I learned of his passion for horses. He'd actually received his first saddle as a Christmas gift when he was seven years old. So I guess it should come as no surprise that once he turned his attention to the Mustang, he would eventually turn to writing about them. As he says, "the story of the Spanish Mustang is also the story of the American West.

The curiosity of a writer can lead to many places. Some seek inspiration in foreign capitals, some in the frozen wastes of the ends of the earth, some in the dark places of the human heart. It is our good fortune that Steve seeks his inspiration in the wild places of the world, whether it is a bass lake, the African bush, or the rolling plains of the American West. For it is here, in the form of a horse known as a "Drinker of the Wind," that we find a living emblem of our yearning to be free.

—Slaton L. White, Deputy Editor, *Field & Stream*

Introduction

The fire had burned low, allowing the dark, star-filled Wyoming night to edge closer to our campsite. When my friend Dick Spencer pushed another log into the coals and then refilled our coffee cups, I knew it was storytelling time again. The others in our group, including the wranglers, had already turned in after the long horseback ride into the remote backcountry area of Yellowstone known as the Thorofare, so only the two of us were still up talking. We were thirty miles from the nearest road and had ridden in for the trout fishing, but that's not what Dick wanted to talk about.

Anyone who ever met Dick Spencer knew about his storytelling. In addition to serving as the editor and then publisher of *Western Horseman*, one of the premier horse and rider magazines in the nation, Dick was also a real-life cowboy who grew up around horses in Texas and then owned a ranch near the famous Colorado mining town of Cripple Creek. He'd taught journalism at his alma mater, the University of Iowa, for several years after WWII, then in 1950 moved to Colorado Springs and joined *Western Horseman*.

Earlier that day while riding together, I'd nearly fallen out of the saddle laughing as he'd related a story of what had happened when he and some other cowboys had "popped slickers" as a sudden mountain squall had blown in on them. The standard raincoat among cowboys in those days was bright yellow, and when four men rushed to don theirs at the same time, the horses spooked in unison at the flash of moving color and bucked three riders into the mud. Dick, a former bronc rider, managed to stay in the saddle.

This night, however, Dick and I talked about wild mustangs, and he asked me directly if I'd considered writing about them. Like Dick, I'd been around horses since an early age, and had received my first saddle as a Christmas present when I was seven years old. I wasn't tall enough to lift the saddle up on my horse's back, so either my father or our farmhand would saddle my horse and have her waiting each afternoon when I got off the school bus.

In the years since, horses had continued to be in my life, sometimes near, other times far, far away, but never completely out of my thoughts. I attended rodeos every chance I could, not only to see the riders and ropers, but also to study their horses. I went on a number of trail rides and pack trips around the country and on one of them I met Dick, striding easily through the Denver airport with a saddle over his shoulder. That's how our friendship began. The thought of investigating wild mustangs had been a distant one for me, even though at that particular time in the late 1970s, there were still quite a few remaining in the West. That evening around the campfire, Dick talked about the history of these unique animals and planted the seed that has resulted in this book.

Here, I have attempted to describe that history, not only in broad terms as it relates directly to the mustangs themselves, but also in short vignettes some readers may consider trivial and unrelated. I have included them because I feel they are also part of the larger story, not only of the horses but also of those who rode them. Long before Dick Spencer and I talked about this book, I had, by growing up in Texas and then traveling extensively for years throughout the West, already been exposed to wild horse history. What I realized once I began my serious research, is that the story of the Spanish Mustang is also the story of the American West, its good and its bad parts.

Wild horses, more than any other creature, stand as a living symbol of that story. Some surviving mustangs have a direct genetic lineage to the animals brought to America more than five hundred years ago, and as such they represent a link to a time in history we can barely imagine. More importantly, because these horses can be brought under saddle, they can take us back into that history with them, an experience whose value cannot be measured. Knowing Dick Spencer and getting to ride with him before his death from cancer in 1989, and adding countless more hours riding in the West in the years since, I feel certain that was also part of the message he was telling me that night up on the Thorofare.

CHAPTER 1

THE ORIGIN OF AMERICA'S WILD HORSES

Horses have been present in North America for millions of years, and as the Pleistocene Epoch began approximately 1.8 million years ago they had acquired the general appearance and body conformation they have today.

Long before there were horsemen, there were horses, and even after the first horsemen started to corral them, beginning about six thousand years ago in what is now the Ukraine, they could not always tame the magnificently maned, long-tailed creatures roaming the rocky ridges and canyons around them. After all, the horses had been ranging free and wild in that part of the world for more than ten thousand years, and in North America for millions of years. Even today, many of the descendants of those same horses, found in the more remote regions of the American West, still cannot be brought under saddle.

The story of these horses is a long one, for their oldest direct lineage has been traced to a small, dog-like creature named Hyracotherium, whose fossil remains, first found near Kent, England and described in 1839 by paleontologist Richard Owen, date back more than fifty million years. Hyracotherium weighed around fifty pounds, had four hoofed toes on its front feet but only three on each hind foot, and probably lived off leaves and plants. It also had the beginnings of ridges on its molars, like today's horses.

In 1876, American paleontologist O. C. Marsh found a full skeleton of this same creature, and placed it in a new genus, Eohippus, meaning "dawn horse." Since the classification Hyracotherium was earlier, Eohippus became a synonym of that genus. Skeletal remains of Eohippus have since been unearthed from Wyoming's Bighorn Basin to the Texas Panhandle. Geographically, the trans-Atlantic distribution of what were essentially the world's first horses occurred during the Cenozoic era when North America, Greenland, and the British Isles were connected as a single land mass; after the continents split and drifted apart, Hyracotherium-England drifted into extinction.

On the North American continent, however, Eohippus continued not only to survive, but also to evolve. The four toes became three, then two, and finally merged into the single hoof of today's modern horse. Some of these animals also became larger, developing strength, stamina, and most importantly, a larger brain that allowed them to become smarter and more adaptable to their environment. In that era, they were still browsers, not grazers as they are today, living primarily off leaves and plants that were readily available during that period. All of this took time, perhaps as long as thirty million years, but the few modifications that did occur in Eohippus are precisely what allowed it to survive and thrive as the world began to change about twenty million years ago.

This was the beginning of the Miocene epoch, and the strongest influencing factors in the horse's survival now were caused by climatic changes as the world became drier. The wet, lush forests that had dominated the terrain were slowly replaced by the vast prairies and grasslands that did not contain the high nutritional value that had allowed the horse to grow stronger, faster, and smarter. Different species thus began to evolve, until more than a dozen different types of horses roamed North America, ranging from the Rocky Mountains to the Great Plains.

Many of the browsing species began to decline, but some of the horses began to adapt even more. They became grazers, developing longer jaws and stronger teeth. They no longer chewed food, but instead, ground it with a side-to-side motion. This allowed them to eat more, and as a result, horses gradually became larger and larger, even though the overall quality of their food had declined.

It is quite probable their digestive systems also became more developed and advanced during this time. Horses today are not ruminants like cows. In place of the four stomach chambers cattle need to break down their food, horses

Throughout their long history, horses have experienced numerous climate changes, and each time, horses adapted and survived when other species became extinct.

have an organ known as the cecum, which works almost twice as fast as rumination. In ruminants, the poorer the food quality, the more time required for digestion, but horses responded (and still do) to low food quality simply by eating more. Today, the horse, rhinoceros, and tapir are the only surviving animals that have this type of digestive system; they are also the only three that have a single-hoofed toe.

Gradually, as the Miocene changed into the Pliocene and then into the Pleistocene, the fossil record of these early ancestors of the horse show they had acquired the basic characteristics of the animal we know today. Even though the climate was changing again and getting colder, horses thrived. Some believe they may even have become more numerous in North America

Initially, North American horses were browsers, but as the climate became drier and forests were replaced by grasslands, the animals became grazers. They became larger and stronger, even though the quality of their food declined.

than bison. Many migrated into Eurasia across the Bering Land Bridge, and as they were crossing, they likely passed the first Paleolithic humans migrating from Asia to North America.

In a strange twist of fate, this westward migration is literally what saved horses from extinction, for between ten thousand and twelve thousand years ago, the animals disappeared entirely in North America. They weren't alone; wooly mammoths, giant elk, and others that had successfully roamed the continent for more than a million years also vanished. While there is probably no single cause for the disappearance of all these species, many scientists postulate that those same prehistoric humans the horses passed while crossing the Bering Strait hunted them all to extinction in North America.

As the last Ice Age ended in North America, the climate also warmed in Europe, and the world's fauna and flora changed once more. This time, new forest growth replaced the grasslands horses had adapted to thousands of years earlier. As the grasses disappeared, the horses moved across Europe into Asia in their search for food. They finally settled in what is now Ukraine, Kazakhstan, and Mongolia where grasslands were still abundant. There, some six thousand years ago, approximately 4,000 to 3,500 BC, early man did not hunt them to extinction, but rather, domesticated them, as depicted in cave art throughout the region. This was *Equus caballus*, pretty much the same horse we know today, although slightly smaller and stockier than a modern Quarter Horse.

Scientists study horse domestication from several different types of evidence, including changes in the teeth and skeletal structure of the horse itself; distribution changes, such as evidence of "new" horses in areas where no such evidence of horses previously existed; and archaeological sites that show changes in human behavior associated with horses. Although some believe that the Scythian culture of Iranian-Eurasian nomads who ranged from western Ukraine to Kazakhstan may have been the first to domesticate horses—they certainly were among the first to master mounted warfare—it is equally as easy to believe domestication of these ancient horses may have occurred at roughly the same time in a number of locations all the way down to North Africa. Different cultures likely traded both domesticating techniques as well as some of the animals themselves, because overall, once it started, horse domestication spread very rapidly.

One subspecies of these ancient horses was never domesticated nor slaughtered to extinction. The animal is known as Przewalski's Horse, *E. feros przewalskii*, and, remarkably, it survives today as the last of these ancient Asian wild horses. About fifteen hundred of them survive, all descendants of a handful of animals that had been placed in zoos a century ago. Although recorded sightings of the horse date to the fifteenth century, they were rediscovered by Russian explorer and geographer Nikolai Przewalski, who described them in 1881. In 1900, thirteen were captured and placed in zoos where nearly all of them reproduced and kept the population alive. They were classified as extinct in the wild in 1969 after the last individual horse was seen in Mongolia.

Since then, international captive breeding programs have increased the population enough that several reintroductions totaling approximately two hundred fifty horses have been made back into various areas of Mongolia. Reproduction has occurred in the wild, and in 2011 Przewalski's Horse was reclassified from extinct in the wild to endangered. In Mongolia, the horse is known as *takhi*, or "spirit."

Overall, the Przewalski's Horse is short and muscular, standing on average thirteen to fourteen hands tall (slightly more than four feet), and weighing up to about seven hundred fifty pounds. Normally brown to dun in coloration, it also has both a dorsal stripe down its back as well as striped legs, characteristics found today in other horses of ancient lineage.

The Denver Zoo is one of several American zoos that have Przewalski's Horses, and one weekend I drove up to see them. The zoo has five of the horses, including one stallion, three mares, and at the time of my visit, a fourteen-week old colt that the staff had named Batu. All five were eating their morning hay when I arrived at their enclosure about 10:30 in the morning. With heads down in the feed troughs, they seemed totally unconcerned about the steady stream of visitors filing past.

Visibly, the differences between these ancient horses and today's horses is striking, particularly in their necks. The necks of the Przewalski's Horses are much thicker and when seen from the side don't look like a neck at all, but rather, like part of the animal's chest. The long forehead and muzzle we're accustomed to seeing in Quarter Horses and thoroughbreds isn't there, either. In its place is a much shorter head, and nearly always with a white muzzle. The manes of the five horses I saw in Denver were all short, stiff, and stood straight up, even in the young colt. Each had a single stripe down its backbone, and all five had the familiar zebra stripes on each leg. From everything I had previously read about Przewalski's Horses, these were near-perfect specimens, seemingly unchanged from their ancestors thousands of years earlier. Primitive is the best word I can think of to describe them, because they certainly did not look like anything I had ever seen before.

Overall, the Denver horses, which ranged in age from eighteen years to the fourteen-week-old colt, were shorter, and they certainly were nowhere as big as Comanche, my fourteen-year-old Quarter Horse. Comanche weighs pretty close to twelve hundred pounds, and he's more than fifteen hands (sixty inches) tall at the withers. Even the stallion at the Denver Zoo, the largest of the five horses, probably didn't weigh more than seven hundred fifty pounds and wasn't much more than thirteen hands (fifty-two inches) tall.

Through e-mail correspondence with Sean Andersen-Vie, media coordinator for the Denver Zoo, I learned the facility has had Przewalski's horses on

The body language of horses, such as one animal acknowledging another's leadership, was probably developed more than a million years ago when horses were extremely numerous in North America. Many forms of their behavior appear to be universal throughout the world today.

display since 1977, and that they are not difficult to manage, quite possibly because the only life any of them has known has been in a zoo environment. Nonetheless, emphasized Sean, the horses are essentially still wild, and any physical attention to the horses, such as hoof trims and medical injections, is done through an exclusion fence.

If there was anything disappointing about seeing the Przewalski's Horses, it was that few visitors to the zoo that morning appeared to understand their significance in the world of today's horses. True, the animals were completely engrossed in eating hay rather than even looking up at the crowd, but most zoo-goers I saw that day hardly spent more than a minute studying the horses and reading the information sign on the walkway before moving on to the next exhibit.

Although the Przewalski's Horse was limited to the Mongolian steppes, once other varieties of the horse were domesticated in the Ukraine and elsewhere, the population spread rapidly, particularly through trade, as different cultures discovered the animal's worth. As it would do some sixty centuries later after it had become reestablished in North America, the horse quickly transformed entire societies.

The use of horses in warfare hastened this transformation, as armies became more mobile and horses could carry more equipment. This was starting as early as 3,000 BC, if not before, across Eurasia where horseback-riding nomads and outlaws soon evolved into more organized armies. Instead of small towns and villages being overrun, the larger forces attacked opposing armies. King Phillip II, who became king of Macedonia, the region north of Greece, is credited as being the first to employ mounted cavalry to charge an enemy. Phillip's son, Alexander the Great, who led that cavalry charge for his father in defeating Greece in 338 BC, went on to expand the Macedonian kingdom all the way to India and Egypt through the use of horses.

Alexander rode a stallion named Bucephalos (also spelled Bucephaus) into battle, until the horse was fatally injured at the Battle of Hydaspes in northern India. Reportedly, Alexander was the only person who was ever able to ride the horse, which knelt on its knees to take his master. Alexander founded the city of Bucephala in honor of the animal, the only city of some seventy that he founded that he did not name after himself. Such was the esteem he held for his mount.

Long before Phillip and Alexander conquered Greece, horses had come to define both Greek and Roman cultures, and the regions' respective mythologies are filled with love of these animals. Their various gods all rode horses or traveled in chariots pulled by horses. Indeed, both societies even had specific gods of horses, Poseidon and Neptune, respectively. In real life, the early Greeks raced horses for sport, and chariot racing was easily one of the most popular events in the early Olympic Games.

The horse's importance to these societies is also reflected in various writings that have survived through the millennia. The earliest of these dates to around 1400 BC, a work produced in Hittite by a soldier and horse trainer named Kikkuli who described a complete, seven-month conditioning program for war horses, some principles of which are followed by endurance athletes today. By adhering to Kikkuli's instructions, the Hittites became the most feared horseman in their part of the world, which today includes northern Iraq, Syria, Turkey, and Lebanon.

While only portions of the Kikkuli text survive, the Greek historian Xenophon's work, *On Horsemanship*, survives in its entirety and is the oldest such work in existence. Written about 350 BC, Xenophon, who was a student of Socrates, wrote a more complete book that instructs readers on topics ranging from horse selection and training techniques to riding positions on both "spirited" and "dull" horses. Xenophon also wrote a second book on horses, *The Cavalry Commander*, which dealt with military training of both the animal and its rider.

With the spread of horses back across Europe and Asia through both warfare and trade, it was only natural that selective breeding was started to bring out specific traits in the animals. Endurance was of paramount importance for wartime, as was speed. Larger horses also became important because of their strength. The equine principle of "form follows function" was closely followed, as not all cultures wanted or required the same type of animal. Some cultures had multiple requirements that required different types of horses.

In the Middle Eastern world, for example, a fast breed known as the Arabian was developed, while along the North African coast, also known as the Barbary Coast (present day Morocco, Algeria, Tunisia, and Libya), a small, fast horse with great endurance, commonly described today as the Barb, was created. These horses ranged from four to five feet tall (twelve to fifteen hands), and usually weighed between about eight hundred and one thousand pounds. The Arabian, which is recognized today as a breed, not a distinct species, may have actually originated thousands of years earlier from the same branch of the ancestral tree as Przewalski's Horse.

In Europe, slightly larger, taller animals, sometimes known as the Norse horse and weighing between one thousand and twelve hundred pounds, were preferred, primarily because of their ability to pull heavier loads. Although considerably stronger than the Arabians and Barbs ridden by soldiers, these larger European horses lacked the speed necessary to become cavalry mounts even though they were certainly sturdy enough to bear the weight of a knight wearing heavy armor. More often, these horses were used to pull supply wagons, and over time, even heavier horses weighing between fifteen hundred and two thousand pounds were developed.

When the Moors invaded and conquered Spain in 711, they were riding their faster Barbs and Arabians, and easily defeated the slower moving Spaniards on their heavier animals. Eventually, a particular province in southern

At their peak population during the Pleistocene Epoch, horses may have been the most numerous animals in North America, outnumbering even bison. In Eurasia, possibly in what is now Ukraine, horses were first domesticated about 6,000 years ago.

Spain, Andalusia, became an important breeding center for the entire Mediterranean region. The horse developed there was a mixture not only of the Barb and Arabian, but also included some of the Norse blood, as well, which increased the animal's size slightly but without affecting its speed or intelligence. This animal became known as the Jennet, or sometimes as the Andalusian, and it is the horse all the Spanish explorers brought with them to the New World, starting with Columbus on his second voyage in 1493.

The horses Columbus, Cortés, Onate, and others brought over from Spain were the finest horses in the world at that time, the result of centuries of selective breeding. Once in the dry climate of the Southwest, the animals thrived and quickly multiplied.

CHAPTER 2

COLUMBUS AND CORTÉS BRING THEM BACK

Sometime late in 1493, possibly between mid-November and early December, Christopher Columbus stepped ashore on the island of Hispaniola, and, just as he had done a year earlier on his first voyage to the New World, changed the course of history in ways no one could have imagined. This time Columbus brought with him twenty-five horses, including fifteen stallions and ten brood mares, the first horses to set foot in North America in more than ten thousand years. During the next three and a half centuries, empires would fall to horse-mounted soldiers and others would rise as new peoples discovered the strange but powerful animals. By 1850, it is estimated that more than two million descendants of Columbus's original horses roamed throughout the western regions of the North American mainland.

At the time, these were unquestionably the finest horses available in the world, strong, intelligent animals with a mixed heritage of more than seven hundred years of selective breeding by the Spaniards. In many respects, it is a testimony to the strength and stamina of these horses that any of them survived the weeks-long voyages from Spain to the Caribbean. On board the small ships, the animals were secured in the holds by slings, or in some instances, simply tied on the open decks. If drinking water became scarce for the crew members, some horses were thrown overboard. The noted Texas author and historian J. Frank Dobie estimated that possibly as many as a third of the horses that left Spain did not survive.

On his first voyage, Columbus had had only three ships, one of which had been wrecked, but because he had no idea where he would eventually land, nor how long the journey would take, no livestock had been taken on board. After he returned to Spain to report to King Ferdinand and Queen Isabella and convinced them of the riches still to come, the king had decreed that henceforth all ships sailing under a Spanish flag to what would become known as the Americas must carry horses, the purpose of which would be to become the brood stock for future Spanish explorers. Thus, on this second voyage, Columbus captained a fleet of seventeen ships and more than a thousand men, and his orders included not only establishing a permanent colony in the new land but also creating special *rancherias* where horses could be bred and raised for inland exploration.

Some of those original twenty-five animals were settled on Hispaniola (now known as the Dominican Republic) near the town of Isabella that Columbus founded on the island's north coast, then later moved to a new colony named Santo Domingo after Isabella was abandoned because of its poor location. Today, Santo Domingo is the largest city in the Caribbean and the oldest continuously inhabited European settlement in the Americas. Just four months later, in April, 1494, Columbus took other horses to Cuba, the island he had also discovered in 1493, where additional breeding ranches were eventually established.

On his third and final voyage in 1498, Columbus added fourteen additional mares to the quickly increasing horse population, and four years later he was followed by Nicolas de Ovando, whom Isabella had appointed to become the new Governor of the Indies. Ovando's fleet of thirty ships carried some twenty-five hundred colonists as well as approximately five dozen more horses. Other explorers followed and all brought horses, so many that the Spanish rulers began to fear their own stocks would be depleted. In 1507, King Ferdinand rescinded his earlier order of 1493 and banned the exportation of any additional horses to the New World.

When a restless, frustrated eighteen-year old youngster named Hernando Cortés had arrived in Santo Domingo several years earlier, in 1504, the *rancherias* Columbus had created were flourishing. Cortés served in various administrative and governing positions in both Hispaniola and Cuba for the next fifteen years, and then in 1519 led an expedition to explore and secure the interior of Mexico for future colonization. He had eleven ships, five hundred men, and seventeen horses, and like Columbus two decades before him, Cortés changed the course of history in ways every bit as dramatic as his predecessor.

Columbus brought the first twenty-five horses back to North America on his second voyage in 1493, landing on the island of Hispaniola. Other Spanish explorers who followed also brought horses with them on each expedition to the New World, spreading them throughout the Caribbean and establishing breeding ranches.

When his horses stepped ashore on the Yucatan Peninsula on March 4, 1519, they were the first horses to set foot on the North American mainland. Despite the fact Cortés had chosen these animals from stock descended from horses Columbus had brought to the islands twenty-five years earlier, many give Cortés the credit for the real introduction of horses to North America since Columbus never actually made it to the mainland.

Cortés had been lured to Mexico by reports of great wealth held by the natives, later to become known as the Aztecs, and within two years he had lain waste to their thousand-year old empire. A soldier with Cortés who chronicled this expedition and conquest, Bernal Diaz del Castillo, also recorded the colors and the names of the horses as well as the soldiers to whom they were assigned. Castillo, who was just twenty-four years old at the time, was obviously a horseman, although he himself was not assigned one of the mounts.

"I wish to put down here from memory all the horses and the mares that we embarked," he writes in his *Historia verdadera de la conquista de la Nueva Espana (True History of the Conquest of New Spain)*. "Captain Cortés, a black bay, which died in San Juan de Ulua (an island in the Gulf of Mexico overlooking Veracruz); Pedro de Alvarado and Hernando Lopez de Arrila, a bright bay mare; Juan Velaquez de Leon, another grey mare, and she was very strong; we called her Bobtail . . ." Upon the death of his horse, Cortés immediately appropriated a stallion named El Arriego from one of his soldiers. One of the mares, a chestnut owned by Juan Sedeno of Havana, actually foaled during the trip across from Cuba.

The horses were brought ashore and allowed to graze for a day, then saddled with bells hung on their breast plates to terrify the Indians when they charged. Whether these bells had the desired effect is largely immaterial, for, as Diaz continues, "The Indians thought the rider and the horse were the same body, as they had never seen a horse," and were awed that the two could separate and then rejoin at will. Later, he writes that the horses "were our only hope of survival" and "the loss of a good horse was more important than that of ten stout men" because the Spaniards were so badly outnumbered. When Cortés left Mexico to return to Spain, his ships are said to have carried not only the Aztec gold he had plundered, but also his surviving horses.

Cortés, Diaz, and the others who took part here were among the first wave of the conquistadors, the heavily-armored riders who conquered not only the Aztecs in Mexico but a short time later the Incas in Peru, and to some extent the Pueblo tribes in the Southwest over the next century and a half. In North America, Cortés was followed by de Soto and Coronado, among others. As these groups moved through the countryside, some of their horses undoubtedly escaped because of poor handling, or just by wandering out of sight.

There is essentially no evidence, however, to prove the specific horses used by Cortés, de Soto, and Coronado were the actual animals that became the progenitors of the wild horses that roam the western United States today, as is widely believed. When de Soto and his men landed south of what is now Tampa Bay in May, 1539, with some two hundred fifty horses, only forty were reportedly still alive three years later, and de Soto himself was dead. A year later the number of horses was down to twenty-two as the few surviving conquistadors built boats and began floating down the Mississippi toward the Gulf of Mexico.

Along the way, when the boats pulled ashore and the horses were allowed to graze for a short time, Indians attacked and killed nearly all the remaining animals. Even if a handful of these horses did manage to survive and escape, there was little chance for reproduction, as all were almost certainly stallions.

As early as 1523, mares had been officially prohibited from being taken out of the islands; Spanish custom at the time dictated that only stallions be ridden, as riding a mare was a sign of humility. Stallions were also thought to be stronger in battle.

In the 1530s, with horses firmly established on all of the Caribbean islands, major breeding centers were established in mainland Mexico in order to supply the next generation of conquistadors. Antonio de Mendoza, the first viceroy of Mexico, is said to have had at least eleven separate horse ranches, and Cortés himself, also knowledgeable in breeding horses, built his own estancia near Oaxaca after returning to Mexico. In 1533, as the grassy plains north of Mexico City became colonized, a royal decree allowed the public to begin grazing their own livestock on lands formerly reserved for government officials, and thus horse populations continued to increase. On February 23, 1540, when a Spanish nobleman named Francisco Vazquez de Coronado began his expedition northward across the American Southwest into what are now the states of Arizona, New Mexico, Texas, Oklahoma, and Kansas, he was easily able to acquire and take with him hundreds horses and mules for himself and his men.

Almost certainly, Coronado also planned to use the horses to pack out the vast riches of gold he expected to find among the Seven Cities of Cibola, which had been described by an earlier explorer, Cabeza de Vaca, and then confirmed by a Franciscan priest, Father Marcos de Niza. In actuality, neither of them had seen any evidence of gold.

De Vaca told his story after surviving seven years of wandering, near-starvation, and semi-enslavement by natives in Texas after the disintegration of his earlier expedition to Florida's Gulf Coast. He and three other survivors ended up on Galveston Island off the Texas coast and then continued westward across Texas, where, at some point along the Rio Grande River, they encountered another tribe of Indians. These natives showed the four men handfuls of shining green stones de Vaca thought to be emeralds, which, he learned, had been obtained through trading with other Indians living in large houses further north up the Rio Grande in a village he translated as Cibola.

This story is considered to be the origin of the fabled Seven Cities of Cibola, for when de Vaca and the others did reach northern Mexico and the Spanish settlement of Culiacan, he immediately began describing the region to the north in terms he hoped would impress the King of Spain enough to send him back. His years-long ordeal had turned de Vaca into a devout Christian, and his excuse for going north was to convert the natives to the Catholic faith, but when he spoke of seeing precious stones, which were actually turquoise, the belief spread quickly that the region was so rich it had to be exploited immediately.

It wasn't de Vaca who was sent northward, however, but rather, three Franciscan friars led by Marcos de Niza. De Niza had been with Pizarro during the conquistador's conquest of Peru in 1533 so it must have been easy for him to spread the rumor that the Indian towns to the north were every bit as rich as those he had seen less than a decade earlier. Spain was in its Golden Age at this time, easily the richest country in Europe (due in no small part to Aztec and Incan gold), and its empire stretched from North Africa all the way to Austria and across to the Netherlands. Colonization of the new land was not on the mind of King Charles, but rather, increasing his treasury even more.

De Niza's small group made their way nearly a thousand miles north from Culiacan to the Zuni village of Hawikuh, but did not enter it. The pueblo's houses gleamed like gold in the late afternoon sun, and he thought he had indeed found the Seven Cities of Cibola. Instead of investigating further, de Niza returned to Mexico City and in his report noted that he saw buildings four and five stories high. Such tall buildings, it was assumed, meant great wealth, and Coronado was assigned to lead the expedition to capture it.

There are differences in the number of horses Coronado reportedly took with him when he started north out of Compostela in April, 1540. One widely accepted report notes that he began with 559 horses and two mares, and twenty-seven months later at the conclusion of his expedition, all the animals were somehow accounted for. This includes those lost in battle, some that were gored during buffalo stampedes, and those that died of starvation, sickness, or other causes. Pedro de Castaneda, the most well-known chronicler of the expedition, wrote that one thousand horses and six hundred pack animals began the expedition, while Coronado himself says he began with fifteen hundred horses, mules, and other pack stock. Coronado's own horse was a black stallion, given to him for the expedition by Cristobal de Onate, whose own son, Juan de Onate, would, fifty-eight years later, establish the first Spanish settlement in the new territory.

Whatever the number of horses, many did not survive, and Coronado, of course, never needed any of them to carry back the gold he was seeking, because he never found any. Aside from discovering the Colorado River and

In October, 1605 conquistador Don Juan Onate camped at this two hundred-foot high rocky butte known today as El Moro, located forty-five miles south of the present-day city of Grants. During a snowstorm, nearly three dozen of his horses escaped and were never recovered, thus becoming the first free-roaming Spanish Mustangs in North America.

the Grand Canyon, his expedition was largely considered a failure upon his return to Mexico City.

Disregarding the report that states all 559 of the expedition's horses were accounted for, and accepting both Castaneda's and Coronado's accounts of traveling with fifteen hundred or more animals, it is easily believable some escaped and became the first wild roaming horses in the United States. Again, however, the fact that Spanish custom at the time dictated only stallions be taken on these types of explorations brings the concept of long term herd survival into question.

At the same time, Castaneda and others describe a winter encampment attack by the natives along the Rio Grande during which some sixty horses were killed, supposedly because the animals were eating the crops in their planted fields. The Pueblo tribes at that time knew nothing of long-term horse management, so it is likely any free-roaming horses from the expedition were eliminated as quickly as possible.

One of the earliest contacts Coronado made with Native Americans at this time occurred near the present-day city of Bernalillo, about fifteen miles north of Albuquerque, where he encountered Kuaua Pueblo, now preserved as the Coronado Historic Site. Located along the banks of the Rio Grande, Kuaua was a large pueblo where the tribe farmed corn, beans, and squash, and hunted elk and deer on the forested slopes of the nearby Sandia Mountains.

The Spanish conquistadors came to the New World searching for gold and other riches, but found little after moving northward into the American Southwest. Their history of colonization is filled with conflict, especially with the native Puebloan tribes who had lived peacefully along the Rio Grande for hundreds of years prior to the Spanish arrival.

Initially, scholars also believed this was where Coronado and his men spent the winters of 1540-41 and 1541-42, but today virtually all agree he actually made his winter encampment somewhere two to three miles further south near Santiago Pueblo. Although the exact location is unclear, that is where the Puebloans likely killed Coronado's horses.

"In all the excavations that have been performed at Kuaua, no horse bones have ever been found," my tour leader, a docent named Georgia Martinez, told me as I walked the grounds. "Unfortunately," she added, "there is nothing left of Santiago. Today, it is a housing development. We know, however, that Coronado and his men, tired, cold, and hungry, demanded food and shelter from numerous pueblos along the river in this area, and even occupied one of the villages and completely displaced the tribe. We can pretty well speculate the attack on his camp was likely by a coalition of the pueblos he invaded."

Kuaua was first excavated in the 1930s under the direction of Dr. Edgar L. Hewett, Director of the School of Archaeology at the University of New Mexico. Hewett believed Coronado had seized and occupied Kuaua, but his excavation showed instead that the Spanish leader had actually spent very little time there. Today Kuaua is best-known for its preserved original Native American kiva murals, which date back to about 1500.

"The entire Coronado expedition, during which his primary mission was finding gold and silver, was considered a disappointment and a failure, even by himself," Georgia said as she showed me the spectacular murals, extremely rare in that they can be viewed by the public at the very site at which they were found. "And as far as introducing Spanish horses into the West," she concluded, "we can't really give him credit for that, either."

For the next four decades, until 1581, there was no further encroachment into the region by the Spaniards, until Fray Augustin Rodriguez and Francisco Chamuscado led a small group of friars and soldiers northward in another attempt to spread the Catholic religion to the Indians. Although they covered a lot of territory, they accomplished little, except that Fray Rodriguez did give the land its name, Nuevo Mexico. Again, some of their horses may have escaped, but if so, the details have been lost to history. For all practical purposes, this expedition, as well as those that followed it after King Philip decided the time had come to establish a permanent colony in the new land, really only served to anger the Pueblo villagers to the point that armed clashes became the norm each time the foreigners entered any of the villages they encountered.

It is easier to accept the idea that Don Juan de Onate, often described as the "last conquistador" and the controversial "founder" of New Mexico, may have inadvertently created America's first wild horse herd during his expedition to the region that began in 1598. Onate had been commissioned by King Philip to convert the Indians to Catholicism, establish settlements, and of course, search for and confiscate any gold and silver the natives might have. Born in Mexico around 1550, Onate had already helped subdue Indian settlements in northern Mexico.

He crossed the Rio Grande in the spring of 1598 with six hundred to seven hundred future colonists, along with a documented assemblage of 1,007 horses, 237 mares, 137 colts, and ninety-one mules, as well as a herd of thousands of cattle, sheep, and goats. Underway, the entourage stretched a mile or longer across the plains. Finding settlements in the area of present-day El Paso, at a point on the Rio Grande known as San Juan de la Toma, he declared his formal possession of Nuevo Mexico. To Onate, this meant all the natives thus became Spanish subjects, and as Spanish subjects, the tribes were then forced to pay taxes—primarily food—to Onate and his colonists.

On July 11, 1598, they reached the pueblo of San Juan, located between the present day cities of Santa Fe and Taos, where Onate halted and settled his colony. He named it San Gabriel. Soon afterward, he began exploring the region in all directions, and on October 29 of that year he and a small group of soldiers camped at the base of a two-hundred-foot high butte, known today as El Moro, located approximately forty-five miles south of the present-day city of Grants. It had been a favorite camping place for centuries because of its reliable water supply, and in April, 1605, Onate would camp there again, this time inscribing his name into the sandstone. But on that October night, a surprise early winter snowstorm swept across the region, and in the blizzard nearly three dozen of his spare horses broke out of the quickly assembled corrals built by the soldiers.

Today, El Moro is administered as a National Monument by the National Park Service. Its attraction is that, in addition to Onate's signature, some two thousand other names of early travelers and explorers, along with numerous ancient petroglyphs, have also

Even though the Spanish Mustang was not as large as today's Quarter Horse, the animals possessed stamina and intelligence, and many of the conquistadors themselves, particularly Cortés, were excellent riders and cared strongly for their personal mounts.

In bringing horses to the New World, the Spanish intended to create *estancias*, or ranches, specifically for breeding. These horses would then be used to supply later Spanish explorers coming to colonize the country. Cortés, who began his conquest of Mexico in 1519, used horses from these ranches.

been carved into the stone walls. One bright, cold January day I walked around the base of the sandstone butte, imagining where Onate might have camped and where the horses could have gone. At an altitude of 7,200 feet, El Moro regularly receives at least forty inches of snow, and October storms like Onate and his men experienced are not uncommon. Indeed, snow from a storm three weeks earlier still lay deep over much of the ground during my visit.

While Onate's escaped horses do not play a major role in the longer narrative of today's wild horses, I wanted to see for myself what might have happened to them. Horses in smaller numbers had been wandering away from virtually every earlier Spanish expedition in Nuevo Mexico, but never so many at one time. The region around El Moro today is relatively open without canyons and arroyos, and thick timber is lacking. The scattered juniper and pinon pine I found around the promontory are much later arrivals.

According to park officials who have also studied the disappearance of Onate's animals, the area then was essentially a high desert grassland with a light pine-oak community growing on the north side. It is easy to believe the horses stampeded on that stormy night, possibly because of mountain lions, known to live in the area today, or for any number of other reasons, and by the time their disappearance was discovered, not only had all sign of them been covered by the blowing snow, but the snow was also too deep and the temperature too cold for the men to try to follow them. Even if the soldiers saw the horses bolt to freedom, it is possible they lost sight of them almost immediately in the storm and darkness. Along Highway 53 on the way to El Moro from Grants, road signs warn motorists of possible zero visibility conditions.

We do know the horses were not recovered, for as author Marc Simmons writes in his highly acclaimed biography of Onate, *The Last Conquistador*, he notes that a few days later, while camped at a Zuni village, Onate ordered three of his men to backtrack to El Moro to search for the horses again.

Thus, those escaped horses became the first documented free-running horses in the United States. There is no record of what happened to those particular animals and it is hard to imagine that they survived long enough to become a viable wild herd. What is known for certain is that barely a hundred years after Columbus had first brought horses back to North America, the animals were here to stay. During the coming months and years of Onate's reign, the Spaniards would set into motion yet another history-changing event for the future of horses in North America.

After Spain's King Ferdinand stopped sending horses to the New World in 1507, the *rancherias* began importing additional horses from North Africa known as Barbs, which they bred with their own Spanish Mustangs. This is the horse the conquistadors rode into the Southwest and which became so well known for its speed and endurance.

CHAPTER 3

DRINKER OF THE WIND

Once King Ferdinand stopped the flow of horses to his New World colonies, it did not take the *rancherias* long to realize the increasing demand for horses would soon deplete both their breeding stocks as well as their riding mounts. They knew what they needed—tough, fast, strong, and intelligent animals that could survive the harsh conditions to which they would be subjected—and the only place they could get them was from North Africa's Barbary Coast.

Within a short time, they were importing Barbs, the very horse the Spaniards had already bred with their Norse horses to create the animals now in their *rancherias*. By adding additional Barb blood to the line, they created what is known today as the Colonial Spanish Horse, the Jennet, better known as the Spanish Mustang. In prose and verse, this horse has been described as a "drinker of the wind" for its speed and endurance, a term that likely dates back to the Moorish invasion or even earlier.

This was the same horse Cortés, Coronado, Onate, and the other conquistadors all rode. The Spanish knew their very livelihood depended on these horses as they moved through the Southwest, which is why the conquistador Juan de Onate sent three of his soldiers back through the snow to try to locate the animals that had escaped at El Moro. The men never found the horses, but by accident ran into one of Onate's most trusted captains, Gaspar Perez de Villagra, cold and starving after days of searching for Onate. Villagra, in fact, had been searching for Onate to tell him of his success in capturing a small band of deserters and horse thieves from their settlement at San Juan.

What Onate did not know at the time was that in the days immediately preceding the loss of horses at El Moro, he had barely escaped his own assassination at the Acoma Pueblo where he had stopped to demand supplies for his own men. Villagra, in his search for Onate, had, in the very same snow-storm, also encountered the antagonistic Acoma tribesmen but managed to escape, only a day later to fall into a deep pit the war party had dug further along the trail. The fall killed Villagra's horse, but he survived to be found by Onate's search party.

Onate apparently failed to grasp the deeper importance of Villagra's story about Acoma, and so he did not send any soldiers out to warn his own nephew, Juan de Zaldivar, who was also following Onate's party with additional men and supplies. Zaldivar and eleven of his men were subsequently killed by the rebelling Acoma and a month later, in January, 1600, Onate changed the course of the history of horsemanship in America when he sent **Vicente de Zaldivar, brother of the slain Juan,** to exact retribution against the Acomans.

Hundreds of Puebloans were killed in the three-day battle atop the rocky mesa, and surviving prisoners were taken to the pueblo of Santo Domingo where males over the age of twenty-five (twenty-four had been captured) were sentenced to have one foot cut off, followed by twenty years of servitude. Younger male prisoners, along with all women over the age of twelve received twenty-year servitude sentences.

This was a completely unknown concept among the Pueblo tribes, and word of the severity of punishment spread throughout the Pueblo world, and indeed, they have not been forgotten today. Onate continued to fight with other rebelling pueblos throughout the remaining years of his governorship until he was replaced in 1609, but anger at the continuing Spanish arrogance in their takeover, their religious demands, forced enslavement, and other fac-tors seethed among the Pueblos for the next seventy years.

On August 10, 1680, the Pueblo tribes, which had secretly been uniting under a shaman from San Juan Pueblo named Pope, rebelled to drive the Spanish out of New Mexico. On that day alone, twenty-one Catholic friars, whom the Puebloans disliked the most, were slain, along with hundreds of Spanish colonists. This is known in history as the Pueblo Revolt, and as then New Mexico Governor Don Antonio de Otermin and his colonists fled Santa Fe southward to El Paso, they left behind thousands of Spanish Mustangs. These horses were immediately taken by the Puebloans as their own, creating a new beginning for themselves as well as for their horses.

From the very beginning of the Spanish exploration and settlement, King Philip II had decreed no Indians were to be allowed to own horses, or even to

The Pueblo of Acoma sits atop a rocky mesa, and in January, 1600, the Spanish attacked the pueblo, killing hundreds of tribesmen and taking about two dozen others as prisoners. Anger among the different Pueblo tribes at the Spanish takeover continued for the next seventy years until they finally drove the Spanish out in 1680.

ride them, but this law was seldom enforced. In some pueblos the natives were learning to ride possibly as early as 1609, barely a dozen years after Onate arrived. What helped precipitate this was the rapid spread of power among the Franciscan friars, who established themselves as the absolute rulers in many of the pueblos as they forcefully tried to convert the Indians to Catholicism. In time, they even began to challenge the decisions of the Governors, starting with Onate.

In the pueblo colonies, ranching and farming became a forced occupation under the direction of the friars, and thus it became necessary to teach their new converts the basics of riding and caring for both horses and mules. This became increasingly more important over the years as a number of estancias were established adjacent to the pueblos for the sole purpose of breeding and raising additional horses.

This statue of the conquistador Don Juan de Onate stands in the small New Mexico town of Alcalde, not far from the site of San Gabriel where he established his first colony in 1598. Later, the site was abandoned and moved to a new location named Santa Fe.

The Spanish, of course, had been riding and training horses for hundreds of years, and for the conquistadors as well as the friars, owning, training, and riding had long been a way of life. They brought with them to New Mexico not only horses but also two distinct riding styles, known as *a la jineta* and *a la brida*. Later, a third style, known as *a la estradiota*, also became widely practiced. Each style had its own purpose, which in turn led to the development of different saddles and bits.

The *jineta* style is thought to date to the Islamic and North African tribes, neither of whom wore armor but instead relied on the speed of their horses during warfare. Riding this way, the horseman sat with his feet directly below his hips, as if he were standing. The knees were just slightly bent, and his upper torso was completely relaxed. This style spread widely as armor became lighter or was even discarded by others since it gave the rider more freedom of movement. *Jineta* training thus emphasized quicker horse turns, stops, and overall maneuverability, all of which were controlled primarily by the reins. This is the riding style used by many on the Coronado expedition, and certainly by those who followed him.

The a *la brida* style was more often used by those who continued to wear heavier armor, and dates back to at least the year 550, if not earlier. The rider sat more stiffly, with his legs and feet extended further forward, braced by stirrups. This is what hastened the development of the rigid cantle saddle, which, with the stirrups, kept the rider in place. Horses trained to be ridden

Many of today's wild horses with Spanish ancestry exhibit similar physical characteristics, including certain markings. Small stripes on the front legs, known as "zebra stripes," are common, as are similar stripes on the shoulders. These horses also frequently have a single dark stripe down the backbone.

this way were totally submissive and moved much slower, due to the weight they were carrying.

In 1550, just eight years after Coronado's failed expedition across the southwest, an Italian writer and horse trainer named Federico Grisone published *Gli ordinidi cavalcare* ("The Rules of Riding"), which became a best-seller across Europe. Grisone advocated a slightly modified *jineta* riding style in which the rider bent his knees slightly and kept his heels down under his hips, rather than forward. The main difference Grisone advocated was in the training of the horse itself, which was much harsher, even to the point of cruelty, to the animal.

Grisone's style became known as *la estradiota*, and it gradually replaced both the *jineta* and *brida* styles in Europe. Today, Grisone's riding style is considered to be the forerunner of modern dressage, which is one of the equestrian sports in modern Olympics. The conquistadors, however, primarily continued to use the *jineta* style of riding and training because it was more practical for their own uses. The horses themselves were also better suited for that style of riding.

The Spanish not only brought a distinct riding style with them to the New World, but special saddles, as well, variations of which are still being produced today for different riding purposes. The *jineta* saddle featured high front and rear arches (today, these are the pommel and cantle) on the saddle-tree with a short, leather-padded seat and a single girth. The high arches formed a type of "bucket" that helped balance the rider and keep him in the saddle.

The *la brida* saddles initially featured a high front arch and much lower rear arch on the saddle-tree that allowed a knight in armor to more easily dismount, or in battle, to slide off his horse. While riding, the rider pushed himself back against this lower cantle by bracing hard against his stirrups. The *estradiota* saddle, likewise, featured a low cantle but a more prominent pommel, although not nearly as high as on the early *jineta* saddles.

Stirrups had been in use for centuries before the Spanish conquest, and when the conquistadors set out from Mexico City to explore and settle the American Southwest, their stirrups were fairly simple and functional. Wood was the most common material although higher-ranking officers likely had stirrups made of iron (silver came later), and shapes ranged from triangular to circular and even trapezoidal. Actual boot support was frequently a rectangular platform much larger than in today's stirrups.

Bit designs were equally as varied, and included the forerunners of today's snaffle, spade, and bar bit designs. Variations of the hackamore were also used, particularly in younger horses whose canine teeth had not yet appeared. A metal bosal was sometimes employed rather than a rope bosal, as well.

Spanish riders have long been known for the ornate designs of their spurs, but originally the conquistadors wore fairly simple spurs, generally made from iron and consisting of a two-to-three inch shank and a small rowel with five to perhaps seven points. They were strapped to the rider's boots, as spurs are today, but there are some reports that after the Puebloans began riding for their Franciscan masters, they strapped spurs to their bare feet.

The Jennet of the conquistadors and its later generations was smaller than today's Quarter Horse, usually thirteen to fourteen hands high but occasionally growing to fifteen. Its head was short and almost triangular in shape, wide across the forehead but narrow at the muzzle. Ears were small, but its chest was deep and its neck muscular. The mane and tail were both thick. The back was short, but overall, the horse was well proportioned and balanced, with overall weight ranging from seven hundred to nine hundred pounds. Colors were varied, ranging from black, bay, and chestnut to grullo, buckskin, roan, and other variations.

When Cortés stepped ashore in Mexico in 1519 with the sixteen Jennets he brought with him from Cuba, he did not think of them as a specific breed of horse, because in those days horses were not classified into breeds. Actually, there was never a pure strain of the Spanish Mustang, and there still is no pure strain today. The Livestock Conservancy, a nonprofit organization founded in 1977 that is working with farmers, ranchers,

Although overall body coloration is not a pure indicator of Spanish heritage, a dark gray body color known as grullo (grulla in mares) with a black mane is common in Spanish Mustangs. Spanish Mustangs also often have a more triangular shaped head, featuring a wide forehead that narrows to the muzzle.

and breeders to protect nearly two hundred breeds of livestock and poultry from extinction, does consider the Colonial Spanish Horse a breed, but one that is made up of numerous distinct strains. To the Conservancy, and to most people who enjoy seeing or being around horses, the Spanish Mustang is the most commonly-used name for this breed.

The legendary American endurance rider, Frank T. Hopkins, who rode a Spanish Mustang to victory in the three-thousand-mile race across the Arabian desert on a horse named Hidalgo in 1890, almost certainly knew the term "drinker of the wind," since he was a strong advocate for the mustang, but he does not use the description in any of his writings. What he did write was that "the Mustang is the most significant animal in America."

Hopkins grew up in Fort Laramie in the years after the Civil War where his childhood companions were Sioux Indians camped by the fort, and virtually all their games involved horses and riding. They were riding Spanish Mustangs, which is why Hopkins often referred to the animals as "Indian ponies." During his life he competed in more than four hundred long-distance horse races, all on Spanish Mustangs. He won all but a handful of them, including his first race, a 1,799-miler from Galveston, Texas to Rutland, Vermont, in 1886. He made the ride in thirty-one days, covering an average of just over fifty-seven miles a day, all on the same horse. The second place rider did not make it to Rutland until thirteen days later.

That victory led to an invitation from Buffalo Bill Cody to join his traveling Wild West Show, which he did. In 1899, while performing with Cody in Paris at the World's Fair, Hopkins was invited to ride in the Arabian three-thousand-mile race, the first time an American had ever competed. He won in sixty-eight days, thirty-three hours ahead of the next rider.

The Livestock Conservancy lists the Spanish Mustang as a threatened breed, and wants to preserve them, if for no other reason than for this dramatic historical heritage. This becomes more important with the realization the Jennet no longer exists in Spain. Estimates of the total number of Spanish Mustangs with a definitive Jennet/Andalusian lineage still remaining in the United States range from two thousand to three thousand head. That there are that many still remaining is generally attributed not only to Hopkins's fame as a long-distance rider with Mustangs, but also to a Wyoming cowboy named Robert E. Brislawn.

Born November 18, 1890 in Sprague, Washington, at the same time Hopkins was riding, Brislawn worked at a number of jobs until joining the US Geological Survey in 1911 where he began as a horse packer. It did not take him long to realize the Spanish Mustang, because of its sure-footedness, seemingly endless endurance, and calm disposition was by far the best horse for the survey team to have. His job required making certain the team had enough pack stock as they surveyed all across the West, so over the years, Brislawn not only became intimately familiar with the Spanish Mustang, he also learned where any that remained could still be found.

The Spanish Mustang has always been admired for its stamina and its speed. The famous endurance rider Frank Hopkins won the three-thousand-mile race across the Arabian desert on a Spanish Mustang, and also performed in Buffalo Bill Cody's Wild West Show on a Mustang.

Brislawn stayed with the US Geological Survey for thirty years, becoming a surveyor as well as packer. Among the areas he personally surveyed was Grand Teton National Park, but in 1941 he was forced to leave the Survey because he did not have a now-required college education. He had long since realized the Spanish Mustang was a disappearing horse, and upon the urging of friends and associates, decided to devote the rest of his life to saving the horse he loved. He started writing letters and contacting friends throughout the West he had met as a surveyor and inquiring about any horses he might be able to purchase.

The first two Brislawn obtained were mares, named Kate and Penny, purchased from neighboring ranchers and both descendants from a herd of mustangs purchased and driven down from the Crow Reservation in Montana in 1925. In the fall of 1945, Brislawn added two stallions from a mustang runner named Monty Holbrook, a man who made his living capturing wild mustangs in Colorado, Utah, and Wyoming, then selling them to ranchers in North Dakota, Canada, or anywhere else he could find a buyer. Brislawn named those horses Buckshot and Ute, and along with the earlier mares, became the founding stock of his own Spanish Mustang herd. He put them on his four-thousand-acre Cayuse Ranch, located near Oshoto, Wyoming.

As he traveled through the West searching for horses, including time in Tijeras, New Mexico, my own hometown, Brislawn continued to study the mustang itself, determined to get the purest animals he could find. He made a special measuring board and refused any horse more than 14.2 hands tall. He studied their ears, bone structure, and overall conformity, but by 1957 he had collected just seventeen horses. That year, he and his family created the Spanish Mustang Registry. Buckshot and Ute, his two original stallions, were the first and second horses registered.

The registry was designed to keep track of the breeding lineage, since by then the Brislawns were selling Spanish Mustangs to others who shared their dream of preserving them by creating their own herds. While Robert was traveling and searching for additional horses, his son Emmett looked after Cayuse Ranch, and after Emmett died in 2010, Emmett's daughter Josie took over management. Today, the Cayuse Ranch continues to breed and sell Spanish Mustangs, nearly seventy-five years after Robert Brislawn started catching them. Their horses are considered to be among the purest of any mustangs remaining in the West today.

To get my first close look at one of these horses, one snowy February day I drove out to La Jara Ranch near Cerrillos, New Mexico, where owners Jim and Donna Mitchell keep a number of Spanish Mustangs, including some they have purchased from Josie Brislawn. Although the horses have more than a thousand acres of beautiful New Mexico hills in which to roam, they are not wild horses. Donna feeds them, and when the horses see her dark pickup moving through their pasture, they come at a run.

Originally from California where she owned and rode horses at a young age, Donna decided she wanted to start riding again when she and her husband

Jim moved to New Mexico in 1990. The only horse person she knew in New Mexico at that time happened to own, train, and sell Spanish Mustangs, and she bought a ten-year-old stallion named Conejo from him, and then added a four-year-old mare, as well.

"That's how it started," she laughed as she threw out the morning's hay for a group of five horses that came right to the truck when we stopped. "We rode and rode and rode those horses, and what I learned from them was that these animals really, I mean really, liked being ridden. They bonded totally with us. That, I realized, is one of the primary and most endearing characteristics of the Spanish Mustang, but it is not true in other breeds.

"Of course, the Spanish Mustang has a very romantic history, which also makes it an attractive horse to own, but I personally think of these horses as an indigenous species, and that they are worth saving and preserving as much as any other species. They learned how to survive here. This country made these horses, and they are the only breed of horse we have not changed. We're not breeding them for a specific color or size, only to preserve them."

To that end, in 2004, she and Doug Lanham of Santa Fe created the Spanish Mustang Foundation. Its purpose is not specifically to breed the horses, but rather to educate and increase the public's awareness of the horse's legacy. Events are scheduled at La Jara Ranch throughout the spring, summer, and fall months, and are open to anyone who wants to learn basic horsemanship and how to communicate with horses.

Seeing the La Jara horses led me to the obvious question: if the Spanish Mustang can trace its history back to Columbus and Cortés, Coronado and Onate, how, after nearly five hundred years, can anyone positively identify a Spanish Mustang today? The answer was just as obvious: DNA testing, and for that I telephoned Dr. Gus Cothran at Texas A&M University in College Station.

Cothran has tested literally thousands of horses around the world during his career, and has established a solid baseline of genetic markers that can help in determining a mustang's background. He is the first to admit, however, that the type of testing done in the various laboratories around the country today has its limitations in picking up an animal's specific ancestry.

"It is difficult to be really precise when testing individual horses," Dr. Cothran told me. "Testing a number of animals in the same herd gives us much better comparisons, but still, when it comes to DNA testing, it is a little more difficult to say anything more definite than that there is, or is not, a Spanish component to a particular group of horses.

"The pre-DNA testing we used to do was blood typing, which gave us a better indication of place of origin than today's DNA marker system does. There is actually a stronger genetic component to the physical characteristics of a horse than there is to the DNA markers, because in Nature's natural selection process, as well as man's selective breeding, certain characteristics are essentially 'fixed' in a breed over a long period of time."

Thus, Cochran has always told people it is extremely important to look at the physical characteristics of the horse. In the case of the Spanish Mustang, those physical characteristics are quite distinct, which, along with performance, are all Brislawn and Hopkins had to go on when they started breeding their own mustangs.

"I never tested any of the old Brislawn horses," Cothran continued, "but I have tested quite a number of horses with known Brislawn lineage, and even though they were always individual horses from different owners, they usually showed a definitive Spanish background. I really would have liked to have tested some of the Hopkins horses, as well."

Cothran, who has been at Texas A&M for ten years, began his horse ancestry studies years earlier while at the University of Kentucky. He became involved in a study of some of the East Coast barrier island horses, and one of the questions that arose concerned the origins of those horses. Cothran had no comparative data at that time, so he started obtaining blood samples from a variety of different breeds, just to create a basic data base.

"During that time, I was contacted by Mary Ann Thompson, the registrar of the Brislawn Spanish Mustang Registry," Cothran went on. "She asked if I could test mustangs, and I said 'Yes'. That was the beginning. Then, the Bureau of Land Management contacted me about testing some of their horses. They wanted to save those animals with Spanish ancestry, so I worked with them and tested their animals in the Cerbat Mountains in Arizona.

"Those first horses I looked at with them were the most Spanish of the ones remaining in the wild, and today they still show the most concentrated Spanish background of any of the remaining herds. Unfortunately, there are only a handful of herds on the ranges now that still show as strong a Spanish background as they did in the early 1990s when I was doing my first testing."

It does not take long to dilute a horse's lineage. At one time, Cochran told me, he used say all of America's wild horses could trace their ancestry to the horses of the conquistadors, but he doesn't say it any longer. Over the last one hundred years, particularly since the Depression Era, a lot of the real Spanish horses were removed from the land so that a lot of what is out there is a mixture of Spanish, ranch, and farm stock that has been released and has generations of diluted breeding.

"Nonetheless," Cochran concluded, "I do believe the Spanish Colonial Horse, where it does exist, is a truly valuable resource and unique in the sense of what it has accomplished since the Spanish brought them over here. Can it be preserved? Yes, but it's going to take a lot of work and cooperation from a lot of different people."

The arrival of Spanish horses changed Native American cultures many ways, but virtually every tribe embraced horses very quickly. The Puebloans, Apaches, Utes, Navajos, and Comanches, who were among the earliest to get horses, spread horses to other tribes throughout the West through trading.

CHAPTER 4

THE INDIAN HORSE CULTURE BEGINS

No one knows where the Apaches came from, or when they first arrived in the American Southwest. Linguistically, they are one of the Athapascan-speaking tribes, which links them to certain northern and Pacific coast tribes, but even the Apaches themselves have no oral history of when they might have migrated into the Four Corners country of New Mexico, Arizona, Utah, and Colorado.

What is known for certain is that in a very short time after the arrival of the conquistadors the Apaches became some of the finest horsemen in the Southwest, the first Native American tribe whose culture, lifestyle, and tribal history was changed by the arrival of Spanish horses. In less than half a century, this new horse culture also engulfed the Navajo, as well as two other tribes in the Southwest, the Ute and Comanche; and as it did, the history of Western America changed, as well. Almost as quickly as they themselves adapted the horse into their own cultures, these four tribes became the primary instruments in spreading the animals up the Rocky Mountains and into the Northern Plains. Unlike the Pueblo, none of these four tribes ever came under Spanish control.

Pedro de Castaneda, the chronicler of Coronado's expedition, does not mention the Apaches being mounted on horseback when they were initially encountered, only that they appeared to be nomadic, continually moving as they followed wild game across the plains. Family belongings were carried from camp to camp by large dogs. Even though the Apaches had been raiding the Pueblo tribes for years, once they began using horses, they continued to not only remain nomads, but also became much more warlike. Raids on different pueblos continued, but later expanded to include Spanish and Mexican settlements, where cattle, sheep, beans, and corn, as well as additional horses could be taken.

The Navajo, who have also resided in the Southwest for centuries, are likewise part of the Athapascan family, so in that way they are related to the Apaches, but in 1540 when Coronado's expedition made the first European contact with Apaches in eastern Arizona near the Gila River, the tribe had already split from the Navajo. A year later, in far northeastern New Mexico while still searching for the fabled lost cities of gold, the explorer encountered another tribe of Apaches, so they had not only split from the Navajo, the tribe had also divided into several distinct groups and spread across a wide geographical area.

Horses not only allowed tribes to become more mobile, the animals also became a measure of wealth. Raiding parties, not only against the Spanish but also between tribes, became more frequent as young men tried to gain wealth, prestige, and warrior status.

No evidence exists to precisely date the arrival of the Navajo into the Southwest, and some researchers theorize they could have been present as early as the twelfth century, and that the Apaches came later. Initially, the conquistadors did not even know of the Navajo presence because of their location far from the Rio Grande pueblos. They first appear in the Spanish record more than two decades after Onate's arrival, when Father Zarate-Salmeron, in a 1626 report to Spain, mentions "mysterious Nabaho" living far to the west and north of Santa Fe. A year later, Fray Alonso de Benevides described them as "great farmers," and named them Navajo.

Navajo oral tradition states that their peoples have always lived together with their horses, and that they came into being together, which makes it difficult to determine when they may have ob-

Because many Indian tribes were nomadic, their horse herds were not kept in corrals. They were allowed to roam and graze freely at each camp, and many animals undoubtedly wandered away to join other wild horses that were never recovered.

tained their first horses. It is probable they stole them from the Pueblo, from whom they also stole their first sheep. Different Pueblo tribes often ventured into Navajo land to obtain flint, and when they did, the two tribes clashed. Certainly, by 1680, they were mounted.

To be sure, the Spanish did their part to aggravate the other tribes besides the Pueblo. When Don Luis de Rosas arrived in Santa Fe in 1637 to become the tenth governor of the colony, he was almost immediately confronted by the Franciscans and accused of leading slave raids against both the Apaches and Utes, selling some of his captives and forcing others to labor in his private shop in Santa Fe. In return, de Rosas excommunicated some of the accusing friars.

Four years later, de Rosas himself was excommunicated and sent to prison where, on January 25, 1642, he was assassinated in his cell.

As with the Apaches and the Navajo, no one knows when the Utes arrived in Utah, but by 1500 they had almost certainly dispersed as far south as the northern edge of New Mexico, as well as into portions of Colorado and Wyoming. They were also nomadic hunters and gatherers, and became widely known for their work in tanning deer and buffalo hides. One chronology of Ute history states that they began trading with the Spanish in 1598, a relationship that soured, of course, a little over three decades later with de Rosas.

At various times, the Utes were also at war with the Navajo and the Apache, and may have acquired their first horses as early as 1637. Not long after their capture and enslavement by de Rosas, a number of the Utes are known to have escaped from Santa Fe, taking horses with them. Once committed to the horse culture, they became raiders like the Apache, and were actually known to sell captives from other tribes to the Spanish in exchange for horses.

The Pueblo tribes of New Mexico, located primarily along the Rio Grande between Taos in the north and Socorro to the south, did not become absorbed by the horse culture, even though they were the first Indians exposed to it. In large part, however, they were responsible for starting it. Just a few years after Onate's *entrada* in 1598, Franciscan friars were formally directed by King Phillip III of Spain to establish missions at as many of the pueblos as possible, and additional friars came up from Mexico City to speed this process, all in the name of converting the Puebloans to Christianity.

This order was followed by special permission from Spain to employ the Puebloans as needed, particularly in managing the sheep, cattle, and horse herds that were soon started at many pueblos. Sheep and cattle were needed for subsistence and horses were used to move them from place to place as necessary. As early as 1610, according to various accounts, a number of the Indians had been taught to ride horses and had become familiar with managing and even training them.

As often as not, horses were allowed to graze freely around the pueblos during the day, resulting in numerous Indian crops being destroyed and thus creating additional hardships on individual families. This grievance against their Spanish masters only increased through the years as livestock herds increased. By the 1620s, many of the different missions owned literally thousands of head of livestock, and the friars had created their own *estancias*.

In frustration and anger, some Puebloans left their villages to join the Apaches, and they took horses with them. Other Pueblo tribes secretly traded horses to the Apaches.

There is some indication the Apaches could have stolen their first horses some years earlier, by raiding Mexican ranches along the northern frontier, particularly in Sonora and Chihuahua, but regardless of how and when they actually obtained their first mounts, they soon became highly proficient in using them. In their roaming lifestyle, horses quickly took the place of dogs in moving the camps, while at the same time horses became regarded as a source of wealth. In the earliest years after the Spanish conquest, the Apaches did not harass the Spanish to any great extent, but this changed dramatically once they began accumulating their own horse herds.

Part of this can be explained by the land, which in turn also provides a glimpse of how horses not only survived, but thrived in the years to come. New Mexico's eastern high plains at that time were covered with different grasses that attracted huge herds of buffalo, upon which both the Apaches and the Utes depended for their subsistence. Because of the long growing season, these were also the best areas for grazing the Spanish cattle and horses. Josiah Gregg, who recorded his observations in his classic work *Commerce of the Prairies* as he crossed and recrossed the region four times between 1831 and 1840, wrote that New Mexico's high table-plains still "afforded the finest grazing in the world," and that the feeding of stock was "almost entirely unknown" in the region.

New Mexico was only a small part of the vast expanse of grasslands covering the country. Known as the Great Plains, the grasslands stretched from the Rio Grande nearly 2,000 miles northward into Alberta and Saskatchewan. Included were portions of Texas, Oklahoma, Kansas, Colorado, Nebraska, Wyoming, North and South Dakota, and Montana.

Thus, it is easy to understand how conflicts between the Indians and the Spanish started and then continued to grow. The Apaches never embraced a farming lifestyle other than perhaps to cultivate small plots of beans or corn, so Spanish cattle represented quick, easy food and horses meant increased wealth and status. Both were also easy to steal because they stayed together in herds.

Frank C. Lockwood, in his carefully researched work, *The Apache Indians* writes that in the mid-1600s the tribe "constituted such a threat to the Pueblo

Once the Apaches gained horses, their attacks on the Pueblos and the Spanish became much more frequent. This is one reason, along with a prolonged drought, that Quarai Pueblo was abandoned in the 1670s. Another nearby Pueblo, Gran Quivira, was abandoned for the same reasons, after being occupied for nearly nine hundred years.

Indians as to halt their natural advance toward the east," and later "made large areas of the most fertile parts of Arizona uninhabitable." In the 1670s, three of the most southeasterly located pueblos, Abo, Quarai, and Gran Quivira, were abandoned; drought and starvation are among the reasons given for the abandonment, along with the constant attacks by the Apaches. Established to mine the nearby salt beds, Gran Quivira had been home to as many as two thousand Puebloans and been occupied for nearly nine hundred years.

The Comanches were actually latecomers into this region, moving down from the Arkansas River Valley of the southern Rockies sometime in the late seventeenth or early eighteenth centuries, possibly by the time of the Pueblo Revolt in 1680. Historians generally believe they already owned horses, having probably obtained them in trades with the Utes to whom they were distantly related. Both the Utes and Comanches may have split from the Eastern Sho-shone of Colorado and Wyoming, and actually formed separate tribes, since today their languages and some of their customs are similar.

As had already happened with other tribes in the Southwest, accepting the new horse culture allowed the Comanches to hunt buffalo more successfully and across a wider sweep of the plains, as well as to raid more often when-ever they needed supplies or more horses. The acquisition of horses also in-creased trading possibilities. Not only could the Comanches travel farther to meet different tribes, the horses themselves could be exchanged for various goods. The Comanches also surpassed the Apaches in their skills of horsemanship, and in time would become known as the Lords of the Plains.

The Comanches are said to have even developed their own breed of horse, a Pinto known as the Medicine Hat, or War Bonnet, that exhibited exceptional fierce-ness during raids and in battle. The Medicine Hat, which can still be found today, is not a separate breed, but rather, a horse with distinctive, almost rare markings, in this case an animal with essen-tially overall white coloration but with brown or black across the top of the head and ears. The eyes are frequently blue, or dark and surrounded by white skin.

Perhaps the Comanches began trying to breed horses selectively for this coloration, but they certainly were not the only tribe that put spe-cial value on unusual coloration in

Many tribes placed a higher value on horses with certain colors. The Shoshones liked paints with a mixture of black or brown with white, while the Nez Perce liked horses with white spots, today's Appaloosa. The Comanches may have even developed their own favorite, the Medicine Hat coloration that features brown or black across the top of the head and ears.

their horses. Virtually all of the Plains tribes, including the Kiowa, Cheyenne, and Lakota, also believed Medicine Hat-type horses possessed magical abilities to warn their riders of approaching danger and to protect them in battle. Horses with this color pattern were highly prized, closely guarded, and always sought after in raids. Medicine Hats are still prized, and are most often produced in Spanish Mustang herds.

Understanding this level and depth of old horse culture is not easy in today's modern world, so I made a trip to Lawton, Oklahoma, where Comanche tribal headquarters is located and where the majority of its members live. There, at the Comanche National Museum and Cultural Center, I spoke with Cultural Specialist Carney Saupitty, Jr. to learn more about the well-documented Comanche horsemanship and how they became such skilled riders.

"During that time, Comanches were literally introduced to horses as infants," Carney told me with an easily seen touch of pride that matched his smile. "Babies were strapped into a saddle on a gentle mare and stayed there for hours. By the time a Comanche was five years old, he could usually ride on his own, with or without a saddle."

He went on, "Through oral tradition, we know that at that time in our history Comanche life totally revolved around the horse. They were important not only as individual wealth like we value dollars today, but as tribal wealth, too. Young boys played games as all young boys do, but for the Comanche, those games nearly always involved horses. They would ride full speed across a meadow, then lean over and reach down to pick up a stick or small pot on the ground.

"At some point, their lives might depend on being able to do that, but only a few of the best trick riders can do that today."

The Spaniards had no inkling of the Pueblo Revolt, so suddenly did it happen, and in a matter of only a few days they were retreating to El Paso. They left behind thousands of horses, cattle, sheep, and other livestock, not only in Santa Fe but also in the pueblos and *estancias* the friars had controlled along the Rio Grande. The Comanches, Apaches, Navajos, and Utes did not take part with the Pueblos in the revolt, but all shared in the spoils, since the majority of the horses and cattle were simply turned loose to roam. Even though these four Plains tribes, along with the Pueblo, owned and rode horses before the revolt, that single event solidified the horse-culture and prepared the way for the animals' rapid movement northward along both the eastern and western slopes of the Rocky Mountains. It also allowed some of those free-roaming horses not immediately captured by the Indians to make their way southeastward into Texas where they multiplied rapidly.

Barely a dozen years after the Pueblo Revolt, the Spanish returned to New Mexico in 1692-93 under the leadership of Don Diego de Vargas. This time the reconquest was somewhat more peaceful, although de Vargas was continually harassed by the Apaches and in all likelihood lost some horses to them. Some Puebloans, especially the Jemez, completely abandoned their pueblos and joined the Navajos while other pueblos were abandoned as the inhabitants relocated to the tops of distant mesas.

Emboldened by horses that encouraged their raiding lifestyle, the Apaches, Utes, Comanches, and the Navajos became increasingly more warlike throughout the eighteenth and into the nineteenth centuries, fighting with the

As the Spanish built their missions at different pueblos, they also forced the Indians to work in managing their sheep, cattle, and horses. As early as 1610, some Puebloans had been taught to train and ride horses. They then passed this knowledge on to the Apaches and others with whom they traded.

Spanish and the Pueblo, as well as among themselves. Truces lasted only until a tribe needed something another tribe owned. The Navajo, who continued to be semi-pastoral and who preferred stealing sheep more than horses, became known for making peace in the spring so they could raise and harvest their crops of beans and squash during the summer without worrying about being attacked. After the crops had been collected, they began raiding again.

In all of the raiding chaos, which frequently covered hundreds of miles of travel, some horses escaped, especially after they had been stolen and were being driven away in a rush. Even when safely back in a tribe's encampment, horses were turned loose, since they had no corrals for them. These escaped animals formed small herds and some of the herds undoubtedly found their way into safer canyons or out into the endless grasslands where they prospered and multiplied. The Spanish named these animals *mestenos*, meaning "wild," from which the Americanized version became "mustang," the name given to practically every wild horse today.

Raiding, warfare, and escaped horses, however were not the only way Spanish Mustangs spread throughout the American West. At this particular time, horses also spread through trade between different tribes. Of the southern Plains tribes, the Comanche became the most powerful through warfare—they had pushed the Apaches out of the region by the middle of the 18th century—and thus they also assumed control of much of the trading. For them, horses constituted the primary currency, and by about 1775, the Comanches controlled trading in virtually all of New Mexico as well as across the southern plains and even into the northern plains. The average Comanche family at this time is believed to have owned about three dozen animals, which means that as the tribe's herds increased in size, moving became more of a necessity to keep the animals in good grazing areas.

Much of the Comanche trade took place in their former homeland, the Arkansas River Valley in what is now Colorado. There, other tribes like the Kiowa met them and began taking their new horses northward to Wyoming and Montana where they traded with the Cheyenne and Arapaho. They, in turn, traded horses to tribes along the Missouri, such as the Mandan-Hidatsa, whom Lewis and Clark encountered in 1804.

Horse trading between different tribes as well as with the Spaniards also took place at specific locations on a more or less annual basis, during which a temporary peace was declared amongst all the participants for the duration of trading.

One of the best-known of these events was the Taos Fair, which dates to the mid-eighteenth century and is still reenacted today. Held at Taos Pueblo, the fair, usually held in July or August, attracted not only Comanches but also the Utes and Apaches, along with Puebloans from nearby villages. Settlers, government officials, and later, Spanish traders, known as Comancheros, also attended.

The Comanches, in addition to their superb horsemanship, were also experts at tanning deer, elk, and buffalo hides, which were highly prized by the Spaniards who, in fact, would take them to settlements in Mexico for trade. During a week of trading, literally hundreds of hides would change hands. Captives from other tribes taken in raids were also highly prized by the Spaniards, who frequently resold them in the slave-trade.

Over time, the Comanches became the most dominant horse culture in the Southwest. Children were introduced to horses as infants, and by the time a Comanche was five years old he could usually ride on his own

In return, Spanish officials and settlers spent weeks in advance of the trade fair collecting horses to barter. Generally, a Comanche had to pay twelve to fifteen tanned hides for a single horse, although the rate varied on both the quality of the hide as well as the type of horse. A gift of up to fifty horses might have been required in payment to the father of a young maiden a brave hoped to marry. Nonetheless, there is one report from later in the eighteenth century of as many as fifteen hundred horses being traded at Taos during one fair.

From Taos, some horses went to the Kiowa (Kansas), while others went to the Apache, who traded with the Pawnee (Nebraska). They, in turn, took horses to both the Cheyenne and Lakota Sioux (North Dakota). The Utes, who also collected horses in Taos, traded with the Eastern Shoshone (southwest Wyoming). The Eastern Shoshone moved the animals to the Northern Shoshone, Flathead, Nez Perce, and Crow (all in Montana). The Crow traded with the Hidatsa and Mandan tribes on the Missouri River (North Dakota). The Eastern Shoshone, especially, were major traders throughout the northern Rockies, as they had received horses early and established their own large herds.

There are no specific dates for these interactions, but by most estimates, all the Plains tribes were mounted by 1760, if not earlier because every tribe actually had several sources for horses. While each northern tribe quickly assimilated the horse into its own culture, only the Crow ever matched the Comanches in pure horsemanship. The Crow are believed to have also accumulated more horses than any of the other northern tribes.

In the early winter of 2015, I visited the Crow Reservation in Crow Agency, Montana, east of Billings, as with my visit to the Comanches, to learn more details of their horse culture and how it changed their lifestyle. For some time prior to my visit, I had attempted to schedule a visit with Joseph Medicine Crow, the tribe's nationally-acclaimed historian, but had been unable to do so due to his failing health. Born on October 27, 1913, he had grown up in a log cabin on the reservation, listening to stories from tribal members who had participated in the Battle of the Little Bighorn; his great uncle, White Man Runs Him, had been a scout for Custer.

As a northern Wyoming resident, I spent many days hiking, riding my own horse, and hunting elk in the Absaroka Mountains, the old Crow hunting grounds, near my home in the upper Wind River Valley. In that regard, I felt that in some distant way I could relate to the Crow's love of horses. Instead of visiting, however, I was still able to spend a full day doing research at the

Little Big Horn College library in Crow Agency, where the librarians gave me a quiet room to myself and pulled one history book after another off the shelves for me to study.

In his own books, *From the Heart of Crow Country*, and *All Time Great Chieftans of the Crow Indians 1600-1904*, Joseph Medicine Crow himself relates different stories of how the Crow might have obtained their first horses. One particular narrative describes a Crow war party led by a warrior named Young White Buffalo that ventured southwestward to the Green River and either purchased or stole a small group of horses from another tribe (quite possibly the Kiowa) and brought the animals back to the Crow encampment in the upper Wind River Valley. This happened around 1725 to 1730.

I personally like this account, because I heard only slightly different versions of it from other sources, and also because I know both areas. On one of my elk hunts, I found teepee rings still in place atop a large, open plateau overlooking the Wind River, and because it's a good place to camp in spring or summer, I can easily imagine that it could have been where the Crow saw their first horses.

Like the Comanches, young Crow children were taught to ride at an early age. Those who were too small to stay in a saddle were tied to it, where they remained the entire day if necessary. In Crow society, everyone rode horses. It should be accepted these horses, as well as those obtained by the other Northern Plains tribes, were the fast, hardy Spanish Mustangs, as there had been limited opportunities for the original bloodline to be diluted at that time. In a mirror-like image of their Southwestern brethren, once the Crow and other northern tribes became familiar with the horse and recognized the advantages the animal could offer, all quickly took advantage of them.

The horse not only offered an improved way of hunting buffalo, it allowed the tribes to follow the great herds as they moved across grasslands. The tribes thus became more mobile and expanded their own territories. In some instances, tribes literally reestablished themselves in new areas. The Crow, for example, in their need to have more grazing land for their herds, had moved the Shoshone further south.

Owning horses also became a new measure of individual wealth and prestige. In warrior societies, as these were, more recognition and honor were bestowed on one who could steal a horse alive than come back with an enemy scalp. For the Crow, stealing a horse and returning with it alive became one of the requirements of becoming a war chief, the last of whom was Joseph Medicine Crow himself, who stole a horse and ran off forty to fifty others from a group of German SS officers while serving with the 411th Infantry, 103rd Division during World War II.

In fact, while there were definite animosities between different tribes, especially over encroachment into another tribe's accepted hunting grounds, much of the raiding transitioned into forays specifically for stealing horses. Young men wanting warrior status had few ways to achieve such status except by stealing horses. Horses thus changed Indian cultures in some ways, while at the same time tribes also adapted horses into their own lifestyles.

The Crow had ongoing disagreements with the Northern Cheyenne as well as with the Shoshone, and an oral history from the Cheyenne, related by tribal member John Stands in Timber in his book, *Cheyenne Memories*, summarizes the influence of the horse on all the native tribes as accurately as real history: "The buffalo will disappear, at last, and another animal will take its place, a slick animal with a long tail and split hoofs, whose flesh you will learn to eat (cattle). But first there will be another animal you must learn to use.

"It has a shaggy neck and a tail almost touching the ground. Its hoofs are round. This animal will carry you on his back and help you in many ways. Those far hills that seem only a blue vision in the distance take many days to reach now; but with this animal you can get there in a short time, so fear him not."

In South Texas between the Rio Grande and Nueces Rivers, the region known as the Wild Horse Desert became a favorite raiding area for the Comanche while on their way into Mexico. Often returning with hundreds of stolen horses, the raiders frequently lost horses that became wild and quickly multiplied.

CHAPTER 5

WILD HORSES AT BENT'S FORT

Sometime during the morning of September 24, 1804, near what is now the city of Pierre, South Dakota, a member of the Lewis and Clark Expedition, John Colter, stood on the bank of the Missouri River waving to his companions and letting them know his horse had been stolen. Colter, one of the designated hunters for the expedition, had been riding their only horse, and its loss to the Teton Sioux that early autumn day was but a preview of what white Anglo-American explorers, fur trappers, traders, and settlers would face during the next seventy-five years.

Colter himself would have more such encounters with Indians during the coming years. Considered to be the first American mountain man to penetrate the vast wilderness of the West, Colter asked to be dismissed from Lewis and Clark during their return trip. He then wandered across the Rocky Mountains alone, trapping and exploring country no white man had ever seen, including the geysers and thermal pools of Yellowstone. Two years later, in 1808, while on a return fur trapping trip, the Blackfeet would capture Colter, kill his partner John Potts (also a former Lewis and Clark man), then force him to make his legendary run for his life across the rocky, cactus-covered plains.

The Blackfeet, Cheyenne, Crow, Sioux, Shoshone, and other tribes that had, in roundabout ways, traded with the Comanche for their own horses through the years, had been stealing them from each other; the coming of the mountain men in the early nineteenth century simply gave them new opportunities. Later, as Westward expansion by the Americans turned into an unstoppable flood, stealing the intruders' horses became only a part of defending their homeland and traditional way of life.

Far to the south in New Mexico, Spanish settlers had already been losing their horses to Comanche and Apache raiders for decades. In a strange twist of history, in the region that would become Texas, the Comanche themselves were in large part responsible for the origin of the immense herds of wild Spanish Mustangs that formed, thrived, and ranged throughout the coming decades over an area that eventually became known as the Wild Horse Desert. Embracing more than six thousand square miles between the Rio Grande and Nueces Rivers, it was a land many would consider a desert, filled with cactus, mesquite, scattered oaks, and not a lot of water. It also had waving grass, as far as the eye could see and in some places almost as tall as a man's head.

Captured horses that later escaped quickly became wild again and formed huge herds. Indian tribes throughout the West that had been friendly with each other prior to obtaining horses, began raiding each other simply to obtain additional animals.

Buffalo were never as abundant here as they were further north, which meant the horses had less competition for food. In effect, it was ideal horse country.

The French found it first, and completely by accident. In 1685, explorer Robert de La Salle, planning to start a colony at the mouth of the Mississippi River, which he had discovered five years earlier, this time missed the great river and ended up some four hundred miles further down the coast at present-day Matagorda Bay. Undeterred by his error in navigation, the French captain set about establishing his colony anyway, subsisting with a small farming operation along with fishing in the bay and hunting on the mainland.

The little colony lasted two years, but before they abandoned the project, they had raised the ire of Spanish officials in the northeast Mexican village of Monterrey, who in turn alerted government officers in Mexico City. French territory began on the east bank of the Mississippi, while Spain claimed all land up to the western bank. In 1690, even though La Salle had departed, the Spanish decided to settle Texas for themselves, primarily to discourage any further westward colonization by the French. A military force, a contingent of Franciscan priests, as well as accompanying herds of both horses and cattle, traveled across the state and established a mission in eastern Texas, San Francisco de la Espada, not far from the present city of Nacogdoches. Along the way, both the cattle and horses stampeded and many escaped, in all probability becoming some of the first residents of the Wild Horse Desert.

Because this first mission lay hundreds of miles away from any established Spanish support, however, the Spanish sent more colonists northeastward across the Rio Grande to create a series of missions, presidios (forts), and pueblos (towns) to solidify their control over the territory. In May, 1718, a site near the San Antonio River at a spot known as San Pedro Springs was chosen for a mission and village, which was named San Antonio de Valero. In the beginning, even with its seven families and some five hundred horses, the mission was hardly more than a collection of mud bricks and brush, but in time it would become the most famous mission the Spanish ever built in the state—a church that became known as the Alamo.

The more prosperous the missions and their attendant horse and cattle ranches became, the more attractive they were to the Comanche, who raided them regularly all the way down into Mexico as far as Zacatecas and Chihuahua. At times, the Comanche might be herding as many as two thousand horses after a series of raids, during which many undoubtedly escaped.

As the mountain men moved into the West to trap beaver, they quickly recognized the qualities of Spanish Mustangs ridden by the Native Americans, and traded beads, knives, mirrors and other items to obtain them. A fur trapper often needed several horses to carry his traps and other equipment.

Horses are far more nervous creatures than cattle, and thus more prone to stampede, whether from storms, at the smell of a wolf or a mountain lion, or simply at the fear of what was happening. Once the horses did stampede, they immediately scattered, and the Comanche often abandoned them rather than use up time trying to regather them.

At night, without corrals, horses were allowed to graze freely, and the Comanche lost more stampeding animals to wind or lightning. On calm nights, other horses undoubtedly wandered away in the dark, thus adding to the wild population in the region. An observer at the time estimated the Comanche owned more than ten thousand horses, which were moved on an almost daily basis as they grazed away the available forage. Other horses, worn out from hard riding and poor forage, were abandoned on the prairies where many joined existing wild herds.

Over the years, practically every ranch along their thousand-mile swath was plundered, not just once but repeatedly. By 1800 there were more than four hundred such ranches along the Rio Grande alone, some dating back more than half a century, and in the Wild Horse Desert country between the Rio Grande and Nueces Rivers, some of the ranches embraced more than half a million acres. Spanish troops assigned to protect these ranches occasionally managed to recover some stolen animals, but by and large, it was a hopeless task. The Comanche simply stole them back. There were periodic truces, but never any real, lasting peace. The full moon of every month, but especially in September when the raiders seemed to mount their heaviest attacks, became known as the Comanche Moon.

In July, 1806, as part of President Thomas Jefferson's initiative to explore the Louisiana Territory he'd recently purchased—Lewis and Clark were still on their return route, and John Colter was still a month away from asking to leave the expedition—a young New Jersey-born career military officer, Captain Zebulon Pike, was sent out to search for the source of the Arkansas River, an exploration that sent him across the Kansas prairie and into Colorado, then inadvertently into Spanish-held New Mexico. Along the Arkansas, he wrote later in his best-selling account of his expedition, he and his men encountered a herd of wild horses and rode out to look at them more closely.

The horses, in turn, ran toward them, "making the earth tremble under them" with such thunderous noise it reminded Pike of a charge of cavalry. Clearly, by this time the wild horse herds had, through both Indian raids as well as on their own, made their way northward out of Texas.

In 1810, Mexico revolted against Spain, and with Mexico's eventual independence the Spanish troops assigned to protect the ranches were withdrawn. Continued Indian raids forced many families to abandon their ranches, and as they did, livestock was turned out to fend for itself. In 1836, after Sam Houston defeated General Santa Anna at the Battle of San Jacinto and Texas gained its independence from Mexico, more Mexican ranches were abandoned. Even these domesticated horses and cattle quickly reverted back to the wild and continued to multiply, largely undisturbed for the next dozen years until 1848 when Texas again defeated Mexico and finally established the Rio Grande as the boundary between the two countries.

One of the participants in that war was then-Lieutenant Ulysses S. Grant, who years later in his memoirs would describe marching through the Wild Horse Desert with General Maxwell Taylor in the United States' war with Mexico. The future Civil War general and president wrote that the horse herds extended to both the right and left as far as he could see, and he was not sure if they could all be corralled in an area as big as Delaware or Rhode Island. Dobie and other historians estimate there could have been as many as a million roaming across the state at that time, but there is no way of knowing how accurate this number is. One observer did describe seeing a herd of mustangs so large it took an hour to pass it, and that he could see nothing across the level prairie except the mass of horses.

As difficult as it is today to imagine herds of wild horses ranging free in such numbers, it is equally as difficult to picture the amount of territory the Comanches covered in their raids. As a youngster growing up on a small cattle farm in south-central Texas, I remember my father and I frequently riding up by tractor or horseback to a bluff overlooking a creek that ran through our property where we would search for, and usually find, pieces of chipped flint and occasional arrowheads.

That bluff was a favorite stopping place for the Comanches, but traveling in a straight line southwestward through the middle of the Wild Horse Desert, they were still at least 275 miles from the Rio Grande, depending on where they were headed. If they had ridden due south from the Oklahoma border to our bluff, they would have already been on horseback for three hundred miles, and if they had come from the Texas Panhandle and stopped on our place, the distance was more than five hundred miles.

Generally speaking, Indian tribes in the Rocky Mountain West did not travel as far as the Comanches in their quest for horses. For them, wild horses were probably as plentiful, overall, as they were in Texas, but they were scattered over a much larger area, all the way from the Columbia River Basin to the Black Hills. There were also many more Indian tribes from whom to steal or trade, as well as from the growing number of mountain men and traders who soon followed John Colter into the Rockies. At their peak in later years, the Crows probably attained more horses, perhaps as many as ten thousand, than any of the Northern Plains tribes.

While trading among these tribes helped spread the animals throughout the West, bartering was considered a necessity in order to obtain other critical items, including food. This became even more apparent once special Anglo-American trading posts, such as Bent's Fort on the Arkansas River in southeast Colorado, were established. Prior to obtaining horses, many tribes were friendly with each other and at peace; after all had obtained horses, these same tribes began raiding each other to obtain more of them.

"No form of property has ever been more fluid than the horses of the Western Indians," writes Dobie in his book, *The Mustangs.* "When they were not trading horses they were raiding them. Next to counting coup, success in stealing horses—not scrubs but prized and guarded horses—was at the top of warrior virtues." Horse stealing became as important for its glory and prestige as for the wealth it brought, since it was almost always done on foot and required not only stealth in approaching but also speed in departing.

As items of wealth, horses became the currency of the times. The animals were frequently given as gifts between tribal members as well as between different tribes to celebrate special occasions. Horses could be used in the purchase of practically anything if the owner had enough of them. Horses also actually increased trading with the Anglo-Americans; the Americans wanted buffalo robes, which the tribes could more readily supply since horses not only allowed them to follow herds faster but also to hunt the animals easier.

The mountain men following Colter quickly recognized the qualities of the Spanish Mustangs ridden by the Indians, particularly their sure-footedness and their stamina. They also liked and often used mules, particularly as pack stock. Knives, colorful cloth, beadwork, mirrors, and other items were easily bartered for one of more mules, since the Indians did not ride them. Frequently, a mountain man needed several animals, including a horse to ride and others to carry his traps, usually about half a dozen and each weighing about eight pounds (including chains), one or more buffalo robes for bedding, and his packs of beaver pelts.

Not all trapping seasons in the mountains were successful, however, and in 1832, two brothers, Charles and William Bent, along with Taos businessman Ceran St. Vrain, tired of the inconsistencies of the fur trade. Certainly cognizant of the gains to be made in trading with the Indians, the men formed a company to build a permanent trading post specifically for that trade. Charles had already made several trips back to Missouri for wagonloads of supplies he was able to sell at a nice profit in Taos and Santa Fe, while William, just twenty-one at the time, liked the Indian trade far better than trapping beaver.

The site they chose was located a few miles north of the mouth of Purgatory Creek on the Arkansas River in southeast Colorado, approximately six miles east of where the town of La Junta now stands. It was a hot, dry, lonely region, but well known and long traveled by a number of tribes, including the Cheyenne, Arapaho, Shoshone, Utes, Crows, and the Comanches. Grass grew for miles in every direction and buffalo were abundant. The Rocky Mountains and their rich beaver streams were almost within sight. The trading post was also along a 770-mile route that had already been used for a decade by white traders traveling between Independence and Santa Fe, and as such had become known as the Santa Fe Trail. With the Arkansas River forming the boundary between American territory and Mexico, the spot was as close to Taos and Santa Fe as the Bents could legally get.

The trading post opened in 1833, and although it was officially named Fort William, the mountain men and traders simply called the place Bent's Fort, and it remained open for sixteen years, until 1849. Constructed of adobe bricks into a large rectangle 180 feet long and 135 feet wide, and with walls

In 1833, brothers Charles and William Bent opened a trading post on the Arkansas River in southeast Colorado named Bent's Fort. Located along a 775-mile trade route that had become known as the Santa Fe Trail, Bent's Fort soon became a major trading center for the entire region, and during its sixteen-year history, tens of thousands of horses and mules were bought, sold, and traded.

four feet thick and fifteen feet tall, it was the only permanent structure along the entire Santa Fe Trail and quickly became the trading mecca the Bents thought it would be. Trading began with the Cheyenne whom Bent had earlier befriended, and many of the most well-known mountain men of the era spent at least some time there, including Kit Carson, Thomas Fitzpatrick, Joe Meek, Bill Williams, Joe Walker, and others. Another who spent time working for the Bents at the fort was Baptiste Charbonneau, whose mother, Sacajawea, had trundled him as a baby across the Rocky Mountains as she guided Lewis and Clark.

The fort was destroyed in 1849, and just over a century later, after careful restoration according to the original detailed building plans, it became part of the National Park Service's National Register of Historic Places as Bent's

John Carson, great-grandson of legendary mountain man and guide Kit Carson, works as an historian today at Bent's Old Fort, which was completely restored by the National Park Service according to original drawings and measurements. The fort played a major role in spreading horses throughout the West.

Old Fort. In early June, 2016, I spent a weekend at the fort, attending the Santa Fe Trail Encampment, an annual celebration of the fort's trading heyday. There I met and spent a day with John Carson, great-grandson of Kit Carson. We had spoken earlier by phone, and he was waiting for me when I arrived.

Carson was fifty-nine that day, and wore his mantel of historic ancestry well, and with pride. He was wearing deerskin trousers and moccasins he'd made himself, which, combined with his slight build, certainly helped him look the part of his great-grandfather. For years he taught American history at both the high school and college levels "with an emphasis on the mountain men," he told me, but ten years ago the National Park Service hired him to be one of their historians fulltime. He is soft-spoken but quick to speak to the fort's visitors, although the majority do not know who he is.

"Horses and mules formed a large part of the Bent's Fort commerce," Carson explained as he led a tour through the fort, "because the post attracted such a wide range of customers. The Bents caught the last few years of the beaver trade, so mountain men traded here, either bringing in wild horses to sell, or trading their beaver pelts for fresh mounts. There was also the Indian trade, especially with the Cheyenne, but also with many other tribes that brought in horses and mules, or needed them. It was always customary to exchange gifts with the different tribes when they came to the fort, just as a matter of good will, and the Bents often gave some horses to them, because the animals were always in demand, whether the tribes actually needed them or not.

"Later, there were the emigrants headed down to Santa Fe or across to California and they always needed fresh stock. The Bent's actually had a monopoly on trade. They controlled everything south of the Platte River and north of the Canadian (Texas Panhandle), out to Kansas, south to Taos, a huge chunk of the West. It was known as an honest trade, too," Carson continued, "probably one of the most respected businesses in the entire country at that time."

Mules, horses, and Indian blankets (today, typically known as Navajo blankets) were among the most important trade items coming up from Santa Fe. A good horse that could be used to hunt buffalo was worth about thirty to perhaps forty dollars at the fort, but the price fell quickly for lesser animals. A worn out saddle horse, for example, might bring only five dollars. Even the wild mustangs captured on the prairie seldom brought more than about ten dollars, since they had to be broken before they could be ridden or packed. By comparison, a good buffalo robe was worth four to seven dollars.

The mules coming through Bent's Fort were not the same mules that had been common in the East for many years. The Spanish mules were almost certainly bred from the Spanish Mustangs, as they were also slightly smaller, weighing around seven hundred pounds and standing about twelve hands high. The animals possessed exceptional strength and endurance, however, and survived easily on the often poor forage available on the plains, just as the Spanish Mustangs did. Early Santa Fe traders preceding the Bents took some

John Carson, left, poses with Jim Sebastian inside the walls of Bent's Old Fort. Both men are dressed in authentic, self-made clothing of the 1830s and hold rifles like those used by the mountain men they represent.

of these mules back to Missouri where they were bred, not only for farm work but also for future packing along the Santa Fe Trail.

"Horses were always important," Carson continued as we stood under the cottonwoods along the bank of the Arkansas, "and there were actually two kinds of horses coming through Bent's Fort, too. One kind, of course, were the Indian ponies, the Spanish Mustangs. In 1834, a year after the fort opened, three fur trappers, Joe Walker, Peg Leg Smith, and Bill Williams, showed up at Bent's Fort with three hundred head of horses they'd acquired in California. Did they buy all of them? Probably not. Many had Spanish brands on them, but Charles bought all three hundred on the spot. He wasn't worried about any brands or markings on them at all.

"There were plenty of wild horses in this area, too, and the different tribes caught them regularly and brought them in for trading. George Bent,

William's son, wrote in his notes that the largest herds were on the north side of the Arkansas, the same side the fort is on, and that he remembered seeing the herds of the Comanches, Kiowas, and Apaches who were camped near the fort and that the horses were grazing along the river for fifty miles."

The other type of horse that showed up at the fort was typically called an Eastern horse, or a "stable horse," which came in with the emigrants out of Missouri. These horses did not do well in the West because they were accustomed to a grain diet rather than the rough prairie grass. They were larger than the typical mustangs, however, which in the Eastern mind automatically made them superior.

Each night, horses were brought into a corral just behind the fort for security purposes. Carson told me his research indicates there were only three

John Carson, left, and Jim Sebastian ride across the prairie toward Bent's Old Fort the same way Carson's great-grandfather Kit Carson and other fur traders would have done in the 1830s. The trading post was the only permanent building along the Santa Fe Trail, and remained open until 1849.

Indian attacks at the fort during its sixteen-year span, and they occurred during the day after Mexican herders had taken the horses out to graze. This is remarkable, given the overall hostility of the time, but it can be attributed to the overall fairness and firmness of the Bents. For one thing, the Bents never traded or sold alcohol to any of the tribes, and for another, William Bent married a Cheyenne woman, so relations with that tribe were always strong. Once a Cheyenne war party stopped by the fort after a successful horse raid on the Comanches, and in a gesture of good will presented Charles with a spotted stallion that he kept for several years.

On his trips back to St. Louis, Charles Bent not only carried hundreds of pounds of buffalo robes and blankets, but also drove hundreds of head of horses he had accumulated during the preceding months. These he was usually able to sell at a nice profit, especially to settlers about to head west. Even though nearly all were the smaller Spanish Mustangs, he was able to

George Bent, William Bent's son, wrote that he remembered seeing the horse herds of the Comanches, Kiowas, and Apaches who were camped near the fort and that the horse herds were grazing along the river for fifty miles.

convince prospective travelers of their value on the rough trails they would soon face.

The golden era of the mountain men lasted only twenty years, if that long, but the contributions the beaver trappers made to America's westward expansion continue to be felt today. Many of them, like Kit Carson, became guides for the wagon trains, scouts for the military, and advisors for other expeditions, since no one knew the country better than they. Numerous modern highways follow the very routes they discovered and pioneered.

Through them, as well as through traders like Charles and William Bent, horses moved westward, as well. The original transaction ledgers of the fort have long been lost to history so there is no official count of how many horses may have passed through the fort during the sixteen years of active trading there, but even the most conservative estimates put the number at many tens of thousands of animals. It is likely the number is well over 100,000 head. No other trading post anywhere in the Rocky Mountains can match that number. The theft of John Colter's single horse that September day in 1804 was only the beginning.

The increasing number of wagons and settlers coming West led to greater violence between the Indians and whites. In 1847, records indicate that along the Santa Fe Trail, some 6,500 animals, primarily horses and mules, were stolen from the settlers.

CHAPTER 6

THE INDIAN HORSE CULTURE
COMES TO AN END

Although many immigrants had been convinced to purchase the smaller Spanish Mustangs before leaving Missouri, others kept their larger "American" horses, as their decades-old tradition of riding and working with heavier, taller horses was difficult to break. As a result, interbreeding with Spanish Mustangs occurred both by accident as well as by design. The Indians stole the larger American horses and simply included them in their confiscated herds; other animals escaped and joined wild mustang herds; and white settlers tried mixing the two to create a larger animal with some of the stamina and intelligence characteristics of the mustangs. All of these factors contributed to the gradual dilution of the pure Spanish horse roaming the West.

There was no shortage of mustangs on the prairies. In addition to the increased numbers of escaped and abandoned animals from the raiding tribes, additional horses were left free when epidemics of disease, particularly cholera, struck different villages. One such epidemic that swept up the Missouri River in 1837 all but eliminated both the Southern Cheyenne and the Mandans; the only way they knew to fight it was to run away, and in doing so, these two tribes alone turned thousands of horses loose.

The growing number of American horses coming along the Santa Fe Trail into the Southwest, and later along the Oregon Trail further north across the Rockies, began with the purchase of the Louisiana Territory in 1803. The first people attracted were adventurers and fortune seekers, largely traders and fur trappers, but the waves of immigrants increased even more after the end of the War of 1812. "The wilderness west of the Mississippi offered an asylum and a continuance of the old life, and many took advantage of it," wrote Alpheus H. Favour in his book *Old Bill Williams, Mountain Man* (1936). "Here was a great domain, a land as rich as or richer than the land they had left, with even better hunting grounds and more fur-bearing animals and only the Indians to contend with."

Long before William Bent lit the match that destroyed Bent's Fort, the growing belligerence of the Plains tribes had become impossible to ignore along the Santa Fe Trail. The Indians had seen the rapidly increasing numbers of westward-moving wagons, and it did not sit well. Horse and mule stock was frequently stampeded—one party reportedly lost seven hundred animals and another 150 head during individual raids—but immigrants were also being killed if they were unlucky enough to be caught away from their parties. Records indicate that in 1847, along the Santa Fe Trail alone, some 6,500 animals, primarily horses and mules, were stolen, more than three hundred wagons destroyed, and forty-seven Americans killed.

Mexico's independence from Spain in 1821 added to the migration, as, initially, Mexico welcomed Americans, particularly traders. Later, the end of the brief Mexican-American War in 1848, combined with the discovery of gold in California, brought still more immigrants. These newcomers had never before seen such huge herds of buffalo or wild mustangs and they shot them both largely for sport and in huge numbers, then left them to decay on the prairie. Not only were the Indians losing their land and the animals upon which they depended for their very existence, they were also beginning to lose their way of life, and in Comancheria, the Comanches reacted accordingly.

During the 1750s the Comanche had likely been much more brutal against the Spanish than history has recorded, and their strength had only increased in the decades since. By the 1850s and 1860s, they probably owned more than fifteen thousand horses. However, in the 1830s, there was another intruder who would feel the Indians' wrath like never before. In 1838, a fresh Texas government had replaced Sam Houston with a new president, Mirabeau Lamar, and opened all its Indian lands to white settlement. As homesteads rapidly spread (even though statehood would not come until 1845), the Comanche attacks increased even more.

Often, the Comanche took captives, primarily women and young children, and on one raid a nine-year-old girl named Cynthia Ann Parker was taken. She would eventually come to love the Comanche, marry into the tribe, and give birth to three children, including a son who would be named Quanah.

Quanah Parker would grow up to become the strongest chief in the history of the Comanche, and continue fighting against the whites until 1874.

"Citing the Indians' cruelties, Lamar called for an 'exterminating war' against them that would 'admit of no compromise, and have no termination except in their total extinction, or total expulsion'," writes author S. C. Gwynne in *Empire of the Summer Moon*, a superbly researched and highly readable account of Quanah Parker and the Comanche history in Texas. "He demanded the Indians complete submission to the Texans' terms—there would be no endless renegotiation of meaningless boundaries—and stated quite clearly what would happen to them if they did not agree."

The result was years of brutal and difficult warfare between Comanche and Texans. In August, 1840, for example, an estimated one thousand Comanche rode all the way to the Texas coast, ransacking the town of Victoria and completely destroying another named Linnville; along the way they captured as many as three thousand horses, which they then began driving northward. There was no formal U.S. Army cavalry at this time, so the Texans fought largely on their own terms. This is how a special law enforcement group, the Texas Rangers, got its start. There were atrocities by the Americans, as well, such as Brigadier General J. M. Chivington's slaughter of some three hundred peaceful Cheyenne men, women, and children at a place known as Sand Creek south of present-day Denver.

Each engagement led to a retaliatory strike by the "loser," but ever so slowly the Americans learned how to fight the Comanche. They began to fight on horseback, rather than dismounting as they'd been doing, and they started using Indians from other tribes as their guides. Thus, they pushed further and further into the Indian strongholds, and following the end of the Civil War, the military took over with troops of cavalry. Then, they took away the Comanche's most powerful weapon, his horse.

The man who finally ended the 175-year old reign of terror by the Comanche was a tough, totally fearless West Point graduate and seven-time brevetted Civil War officer named Ranald Slidell Mackenzie. He graduated first in his class at West Point in 1862, served at Chancellorsville, Gettysburg, and Cold Harbor, and had been wounded six times. After the war, in 1871, he assumed command of the Fourth Cavalry at Fort Concho near present-day San Angelo, Texas. Ulysses S. Grant, William T. Sherman, and Philip Sheridan, the men who had led the Union in its defeat of the Confederacy, now ran the country as well as its military, and they set their compass toward the West with the goal of total defeat of the Indians. This meant not just the Comanche but all the Plains tribes, and Mackenzie fit well into their plans.

On his first foray afield, however, Mackenzie promptly had more than sixty horses stolen by Quanah Parker and his warriors, including his own favorite mount. Mackenzie responded by chasing the Comanche for nearly fifty miles through the Llano Estacado Plains, into and down steep, winding canyons, then back up on the wide open plains again. Finally, in the face of a driving blizzard, he abandoned his pursuit. It was the first time any opposing force had so penetrated Comancheria.

Mackenzie's next opportunity came a year later in September, 1872. He surprised a Comanche camp—this time his guide was a Comanchero trader from New Mexico—on the North Fork of the Red River—and not only killed more than fifty Indians but also captured some three thousand Indian ponies. Everything else in the camp was burned. That night, surviving Comanches raided back and recovered nearly all the animals.

The final blow came southeast of present-day Amarillo on September 28, 1874, at Palo Duro Canyon, an eight hundred-foot deep, 120-mile long canyon that cuts sharply and unexpectedly through the flat prairie. Shortly after dawn, Mackenzie and his troops attacked a mixed encampment of Kiowa and Comanche, scattering them, burning the village, and capturing as many as two thousand horses. Remembering his mistake of a year earlier on the North Fork, this time Mackenzie took the captured horses to nearby Tule Canyon and ordered them shot. Without their horses and with their village and winter food supply destroyed, the Comanche and Kiowas soon turned themselves into the reservation at Fort Sill in Oklahoma.

Mackenzie wasn't the first Army officer to use the tactic of slaughtering Indian ponies to help defeat them. A decade earlier, Kit Carson, appointed a colonel of New Mexico Volunteers and ordered to subdue both the Mescalero Apaches and the Navajos, killed both their horses and sheep, but the record is based almost entirely on Navajo oral tradition and actual numbers are unknown. Carson's personal correspondence to his superior officers in Santa Fe, while describing his successes in the field, do not mention any large numbers of horses captured or destroyed; in fact, he rarely mentions horses at all.

The frontiersman employed the Navajo's traditional enemies, the Ute, Hopi, and Zuni as his scouts, and paid them with captured horses as part of the spoils of war. The government was willing to pay $20 per captured horse, but the Utes, especially, preferred the animals, and again, there is no official account of how many they may have acquired during the six-month campaign. As the Navajo fled ahead of Carson's advance, they abandoned small groups of animals at a time, never the large numbers like Mackenzie would capture at once.

As he followed the Navajos, Carson subdued them more effectively by starving them—burning their corn and wheat fields along with their prized grove of peach trees in Canyon de Chelly. A number of horses likely starved, too. Without food, and no opportunity to obtain any, the Navajos had little option but to surrender. On their infamous Long Walk to Fort Sumner and Bosque Redondo in eastern New Mexico (about 450 miles), they were allowed to take hundreds of their remaining horses and sheep with them, however. An official census conducted at the end of December, 1864 by Captain Francis

In 1864 Kit Carson subdued the Navajos and moved them to Bosque Redondo, a special reservation in eastern New Mexico, more than four hundred miles from their Arizona homeland. Carson defeated the Navajo by burning their crops.

Partially restored walls show the outline of the military buildings at Bosque Redondo. The Navajos were allowed to bring many of their horses with them on the Long Walk to the reservation. A late 1864 census at Bosque Redondo counted 3,038 horses owned by 8,354 Navajos imprisoned there.

McCabe who was stationed at Fort Sumner with the 1st Cavalry of the New Mexico Volunteers, lists 3,038 horses, 143 mules, and 6,962 sheep at Bosque Redondo by the 8,354 Navajos held there.

Later in this same report, prepared for Brigadier General James H. Carleton, Commander of the Military Department of New Mexico and the architect of the Bosque Redondo Reservation, McCabe writes,

Large herds of wild horses run on the Staked Plain, about 50 miles from this, and several warriors who left the reservation with permission to hunt captured a great many of these animals last summer. The horses belonging to the tribe are of a small but well-formed breed, very hardy, and sometimes possessing great speed and power of endurance. In their forays upon the settlements the marauders were enabled to defy their pursuers owing to the good quality of their horses. They will average 12 hands in height, and require little or no grain, but obtain their support from the nutritious gama (sic) grass that abounds in the neighborhood of the reservation. As there is a great proportion of mares among them, a few years will develop a large increase of this species of stock; and it is not going too far to predict that at no distant day our cavalry in this department may be entirely remounted on horses of the Navajo breed.

Visitors to the Bosque Redondo Memorial today, located a few miles south-east of the town of Fort Sumner, find it difficult to get a clear picture of just how bleak conditions were for the Navajos and Apaches, despite having their horses and sheep with them. The grounds are well-kept and a sparkling visitor center includes a remarkable museum that tells the fort's fateful story. The bleakness actually begins right outside town, where the open, treeless countryside begins and extends for forty miles in every direction. That was the size of the original Bosque Redondo Reservation created by Carleton, who was consumed with the concept of dismantling the cultures of both the Apaches and Navajos and turning them into farmers. He had Fort Sumner built specifically for that purpose, and it failed in every respect.

"Carson was reluctant to accept Carleton's assignment, but the General would not accept his resignation," explained Aaron Roth, the Historic Site Manager for Bosque Redondo, when I visited the Memorial one warm June weekend. "Fort Sumner was not designed to be a military fort for the defense of wagon trains and settlers coming through the area like the other forts were. This place was chosen because of its isolation.

"Carleton underestimated the number of Navajos Carson would bring in, so there was seldom enough food for them, and the water in the Pecos River was so alkaline it made the Indians and soldiers alike sick much of the time. I think the only reason their horses survived was because they didn't need grain like the military horses did, but even they had a difficult time. Those that had been injured or were in especially poor conditions were destroyed and issued to the Indians for food."

In 1868, learning of Carleton's mistreatment of the Navajos, General Sherman made a personal visit to the reservation and was appalled at what he saw. Carleton was relieved of duty, the Navajos were allowed to return to their homeland in Arizona, and Fort Sumner was abandoned.

The regular Army officer who does appear to have started killing Indian horses, at least on a large scale, was one of Mackenzie's classmates at West Point, George Armstrong Custer, who on November 27, 1868, ordered between six hundred and eight hundred Cheyenne horses shot after his

One way the United States Army defeated the different tribes and forced them onto reservations was by destroying their horses. George Armstrong Custer, after attacking a peaceful winter encampment of Southern Cheyennes on the Washita River in Oklahoma, destroyed between six hundred and eight hundred of their horses.

7th Cavalry's brief, hour-long engagement on the Washita River in Oklahoma. Custer had attacked and wiped out a peaceful winter encampment of Southern Cheyenne under the leadership of Chief Black Kettle. Officers and scouts were allowed to keep any captured horses they wanted, the fifty-three captive women and children took one each, and the remainder were destroyed.

Destroying Indian horses not only took away a tribe's mobility but also left a sudden and completely unfamiliar void in their society. Their entire value system, their trading capital, and their pride of ownership were taken away, usually within a matter of a few hours. Joseph Medicine Crow of the Crows described this void as being worse than a military defeat, and it was certainly more painful when the Indians had to watch. The soldiers assigned to the task must have also found it wrenching, although in Custer's case, giving the order may not have been that difficult. Although he himself reportedly rode a Thoroughbred and had a second one available in the 7th's remuda, testimonies abound from Custer's men describing his complete disregard for the welfare of both his men and their horses.

Moving northward into Kansas after the Black Kettle fight, so many of the 7th Cavalry's horses died of exposure and starvation and others were in such poor condition that more than five hundred of Custer's eight hundred men were on foot. Mules also died, so many that Custer had to burn most of his supply wagons because there was nothing left to pull them. Eight years later, after Custer's fall at the Little Bighorn, Gall, one of the Sioux chieftains who led the main attack on Custer, said his braves had no difficulty in catching the 7th's horses, but that a few days after the battle they abandoned a lot of them because they were not in very good condition.

Spanish Mustangs like the kind that Indians rode saw limited service in the Cavalry after the Civil War, due to their smaller size, but the horses were used during the war. Horse traders, usually called "mustangers," captured wild mustangs on the prairies and shipped them to both Union and Confederate forces. Although mustangers, both Mexican and American, had been capturing wild mustangs since around 1800 and trading them around the country, ranchers in the post-war West discovered that breeding a Spanish Mustang with an American horse produced a horse with the proper size, stamina, and personality suitable not only for their growing cattle industry but also for the cavalry. The best combination was considered to be a second or third generation animal that was three-quarters American and one-quarter Spanish. This was haphazard breeding at best, in which an American stallion was turned loose into a pasture to breed with mustang mares.

Captain Myles Keogh's famous horse, Comanche, who survived the battle at the Little Bighorn, was one of these American/mustang mixes, purchased by the Army at St. Louis on April 3, 1868. Cavalry records listed him as light bay, weighing 925 pounds and standing fifteen hands high, measurements definitely larger than a standard Spanish Mustang. Keogh, an experienced rider and horseman, then purchased Comanche from the Army as his personal mount for $90, the same amount the Army had paid for the horse.

With the defeat of the various tribes by the United States Army between 1865 and 1890, the Indians were moved to reservations, and with few exceptions, lost the majority of their horses. In some instances, when the Indians formally surrendered, they brought their horse herds with them to the surrender; Chief Crazy Horse, who had helped lead the Sioux in their annihilation of Custer at the Little Bighorn, is said to have brought twelve hundred horses with him to the Red Cloud Agency in what is now Nebraska on May 6, 1877. The military either shot or confiscated the animals, using the excuse that the tribes no longer needed them since they weren't supposed to leave their reservations.

During this time, wild Spanish Mustangs still ran free in both the Wild Horse Desert and in the Llano Estcado of Texas where the mustangers did much of their work. Ranches were being established in both regions years before the Comanche threat had been eliminated, including both the huge

To the Indian tribes, horses were as important as the bison. Horses allowed them to follow the migrating herds and also to hunt them more efficiently. When the buffalo were gone and the tribes moved to different reservations, their horses were often confiscated and then destroyed.

Richard King and Miflin Kenedy Ranches (1853 and 1854, respectively); King reportedly bought part of his holdings, some 15,500 acres, for less than two cents an acre from Mexican landowners who had fled the Comanches.

As he was starting his cattle empire, King paid $6 a head for mustang mares he then bred with American stallions he'd purchased for $200 from the East. By 1874, he was reported to own more than fifty thousand head of cattle and six thousand horses. Sixty years later, Richard King's grandson Robert J. Kleberg, Jr., who with his brother Richard was then running the ranch, would develop the King Ranch Quarter Horse, renowned for its instinctive ability to work cattle. Then they would turn their attention to producing prized Thoroughbreds, one of which, Assault, would win the Triple Crown in 1946.

As cattle became increasingly more important throughout the West, wild mustangs assumed a new role, as J. R. Blocker writes in *The Trail Drivers of Texas*, a collection of experiences written by the trail driving cowboys themselves and compiled and edited by J. Marvin Hunter: "Mustangs furnished mounts for the cowman, and these horses proved their value as an aid to the development of the cattle industry. A good rider could break a mustang to the saddle in a very short time, and for endurance these Spanish ponies had no equal."

Prior to the Civil War, and particularly between 1848 and 1854, both horses and cattle were driven from Texas westward to California and then later to Nevada when the first silver strike in America, the famous Comstock Lode, was discovered in 1859. With demand so high, mustangers increased their efforts to capture the wild horses. More were moved northward and westward after the war as Texas ranchers began driving huge herds of cattle and horses to northern railheads, primarily in Abilene or Dodge City, Kansas, or occasionally to more fertile pastures in Wyoming and Montana.

These cattle drives frequently included as many as three thousand head of cattle along with fifty or more horses, since each cowboy generally had at least five or more animals to ride during the months-long drives. (There were also occasional horse drives, as well, as ranchers found markets for them around the country.) Oliver Loving is credited with making the first cattle drive of this type, taking a herd from Texas all the way to Chicago in 1858. The heyday lasted from about 1870 to 1885, ending when the railroads reached towns closer to the Texas ranches. Personal accounts by the trail drivers from throughout this period frequently describe encounters

The US Cavalry seldom used Spanish Mustangs following the Civil War because the horses were considered to be too small. Ranchers, however, frequently turned their own mares loose to join wild horse herds, letting them breed to obtain the proper size, stamina, and personality they desired.

with wild Spanish Mustangs, along with their generally futile attempts to capture one.

"One day I ran across a party of men in camp who were making the capturing of these mustangs a business," relates John B. Conner, a nineteen-year old cowboy seeing his first mustangers in the Texas Panhandle. "They had several head tethered nearby which they had just captured, and showed me a large bunch standing about a mile away which they informed me they had been running for several days.

"These men worked in relays, and kept the mustangs on the go, without permitting them to rest or get to watering places. The men told me they kept just in sight of them to keep them on the run all day, and finally ran them down. The captured horses I saw there were all beauties."

The trail drivers also describe the hardships faced by their own horses. Sol West, in 1874 at the age of twenty, was contracted to move a herd from Port

Lavaca in the South Texas Wild Horse Desert, to Ellsworth, Kansas. Nine days into the drive, in what is now Oklahoma, he and his men ran head-on into a blizzard. Horses, including his own, actually froze to death with their riders on them, writes West, and during the night all seventy-eight head of their horses perished in the storm that left snow, sleet, and ice a foot and a half deep.

Stampedes, particularly at night, were another constant threat along the trail, and not all of the horses were always recovered. These animals did not help or become the property of the Plains tribes, however, all of whom were struggling to survive the new culture being forced upon them. Of all the Indian tribes to lose their horses, the Crow were perhaps the luckiest, at least in being able to keep their horses for a few more years. This may have been because they had served as scouts for the U.S. Army during the 1876 war against the Sioux and Cheyenne. Even after ceding part of their reservation back to

Many cowboys preferred to use Spanish Mustangs because of their endurance during their long cattle drives northward from Texas. During the drives, even as late as the 1880s, they often reported seeing large herds of wild mustangs in north Texas, Oklahoma, and Colorado.

In the early 1920s, the United States government destroyed more than forty thousand horses belonging to the Crow Indians in Montana. The agents were paid a bounty of $4 per horse, and it took them several years to eliminate the animals.

the United States in 1882, the Crow were still allowed to raise horses, even though their herds were rapidly growing and becoming increasingly wilder.

Around 1919, however, the United States government ordered the tribe to reduce its herds. The reason given was that non-tribal cattlemen who had acquired grazing permits on the reservation felt that the wild Crow ponies were depleting the forage needed for their cattle. The Crow, of course, never removed a single horse, but several years later, government contractors came in and shot the animals at a bounty of $4 per horse. It took them three years, but in the end, more than forty thousand Crow horses, including many with a direct Spanish Mustang lineage, were destroyed.

Many more thousands of mustangs would be captured and killed in coming years. The real fight to save them was only just getting started.

The beginning of the automotive age coincided with the development of mechanized farm machinery to change the future of wild horses. Wild mustangs were eliminated in many areas, and surviving herds were pushed into remote regions.

CHAPTER 7

THE BUREAU OF LAND MANAGEMENT TAKES OVER

The end of the Indian wars coincided with a number of factors that changed, or in many cases strengthened, the attitudes Americans held toward wild mustangs. Among these factors were increased Westward migration and settlement; the development of both automobiles and mechanized farm machinery that replaced horses; the demand for American animals to satisfy European war needs; and finally, the emergence and growth of a new industry to supply canned food for household pets.

The net result of these factors was a loss of probably half of America's free-roaming wild horses across the West in a period of two decades. Wild mustangs were eliminated in many places, and surviving herds were pushed into remote areas where it was just too difficult to catch them. For the most part, this is where the remaining wild herds still exist today.

Westward migration had been going on in one form or another since the early 1800s, but immigrants had received an added incentive with the passage of the Homestead Act, signed into law by President Abraham Lincoln on May 20, 1862. Designed to encourage settlement of the West, the Homestead Act provided settlers with 160 acres of public land for the cost of a simple filing fee. In 1909 the Enlarged Homestead Act doubled the amount of land to 320 acres, and in 1916, the Stock-Raising Amendment doubled the total again to a substantial 640 acres. Any adult who had never taken up arms against the United States Government could file for land, a provision that brought waves of foreign immigrants into the country.

Over the decades, literally millions of acres of land west of the Mississippi were homesteaded and turned into farms where cattle and sheep were soon grazing. Frequently, the homesteaders allowed their stock to graze off their actual deeded property, especially if it was still unclaimed public land. Wild mustangs were considered to be competitors for the available forage and were rounded up and sold. More than 400,000 were reportedly sold to the British for use in the Boer Wars between 1880 and 1902, and, writes J. Edward de Steiguer in *Wild Horses of the West,* 350,000 more were sent to the European front in 1916 in World War I.

During this same time, America was also becoming mechanized. In 1892, John Froelich of Froelich, Iowa, invented the first gasoline-powered tractor. It became the centerpiece of the Waterloo Gasoline Engine Company, and after steady improvements along with a growing audience of receptive Midwest farmers, the company was sold to Deere and Company, a long-established manufacturer of plows, wagons, and buggies that was looking to get into the tractor business. Today, the firm is internationally known for its distinctive green and yellow John Deere brand of farm and yard machinery.

Prior to Froelich's use of a gasoline engine to power his tractor, similar machines had been powered by steam engines. This also happened in automobiles, the first of which in the United States was a steam-powered carriage invented in 1871 by Dr. J. W. Carhart in Racine, Wisconsin. Four years later, perhaps seeing the future of such machines, the State of Wisconsin offered a $10,000 award to the first person to develop a vehicle that could become a substitute for horses.

The proving ground was to be a two-hundred-mile race in which the winner was required to maintain an average speed of more than five miles per hour. Seven vehicles entered but only two started the Green Bay-to-Madison race on July 16, 1878. The winner finished in thirty-three hours, twenty-seven minutes, for an average speed of six miles an hour. Just fifteen years later, in 1893, Charles and Frank Duryea opened the first American automobile manufacturing facility for vehicles using gasoline-powered engines.

Both of these inventions had a major impact on the future of America's wild horses. The tractor was easy to operate, reduced manpower hours in the field, and increased overall farm production. The automobile was quicker, could carry several passengers at once, and did not need grazing space. "The time of the horse's greatest usefulness is past, and the only solution of the horse problem will be found in introducing the meat as an edible," wrote the *New York Times* in 1895, ironically forecasting the next and perhaps most serious threat wild mustangs had yet faced.

Horse meat had been part of the human diet for thousands of years, but during the French Revolution of 1788-1804 when beef became difficult to obtain, horses were eaten in such large numbers the meat became the country's favorite and remained so for much of the nineteenth century. Horse meat never became as popular in the United States, but American butchers did capitalize on the European market. Horses could be purchased for less than $10 per head and the meat easily exported for pennies; one New York butcher, Henry Bosse, is reported to have exported 110,000 pounds of horse meat per month in 1891, netting a profit up to $1,000 per week.

Bosse's success led to the opening of slaughterhouses in Western states, where some firms paid only $3 per horse. Even at that price, mustanging was still a profitable business and continued to be practiced. One of the most successful was a Nevada wrangler named Charles "Pete" Barnum, who is said to have captured more than fourteen thousand mustangs in the state between 1904 and 1920. *Life* Magazine described him as the "King of the Wild Horse Catchers," and Barnum himself wrote about his mustanging in both *Sunset Magazine* and the *Denver Republican*.

In Portland, Oregon, E. E. Schlesser and his brother C. C. opened a slaughterhouse and shipping business named Schlesser Brothers. Originally, they were in the beef business but then changed to horses after a promoter convinced them to switch. Wild horses were brought in by train and were kept in corrals behind the plant. Schlesser Brothers would slaughter as many as one hundred animals a day, put the meat into barrels, and ship them to New York where they were then sent to Holland for human consumption.

While Americans may not have eaten a lot of horse meat during the first half of the twentieth century, their pets did, which led to still another threat for the West's wild mustangs. Starting in the 1920s, the canning market emerged in which wild horses were slaughtered for dog and cat food. Schlesser Brothers was part of this business, as well, and built a separate processing plant adjacent to their original facility where horse meat was canned under the label of "Mankind Dog Food."

Edward Schlesser, son of the company's founder, remembered sitting on the corral fence during the summer before he became an employee and picking out good-looking horses to ride. These were largely wild mustangs and none could be ridden immediately, so he'd work with an animal until he could put a saddle on it, then train it for riding. When the horse was ready, Edward would purchase it from his father for $40, then try to sell it, sometimes collecting as much as $300 for the animal.

According to de Steiguer's well-documented research, in 1935 some two hundred firms in the United States were producing pet food from slaughtered horses, most of which were wild mustangs. California was home to many of the largest pet food companies, including the Ross Dog and Cat Food Company of Los Alamitos, which claimed to have been the first and largest operator on the West Coast. Some of these canning firms even hired out-of-work cowboys to do their roundups for them, and their own horses were supplemented by using airplanes to drive the panic-stricken horses into specially-built traps. By 1937, one of the largest of these firms, CBC, was estimated to have shipped some forty thousand horses to slaughter.

Still another incentive to remove wild, free-roaming horses came in 1934 when Congress passed the Taylor Grazing Act, a bill designed to reduce over-grazing and soil erosion caused by the same cattle and sheep the government had long been promoting through the different homestead acts. The Act created grazing districts that were then divided into smaller tracts known as allotments. Livestock owners became licensees and received ten-year contracts on their allotments, as well as the right to fence them even though the allotments were still public land. In the minds of the licensees, wild mustangs, now fenced in, competed directly with cattle for the available forage and had to be eliminated. The program was administered by the U.S. Grazing Service, which merged with the U.S. General Land Office in 1946 and was renamed the Bureau of Land Management, under the direction of the Department of the Interior.

After WWII, the pet food canning industry surged again. In less than five years following the end of the war, Nevada's Bureau of Land Management allowed approximately a hundred thousand wild mustangs to be removed for the canning industry. That is when, one spring day in 1950, a Reno, Nevada-based insurance agency secretary named Velma Johnston noticed blood dripping from a trailer being pulled through town. Getting a closer look into the trailer when it pulled into the Sparks stockyards several miles outside town, she was stunned to see it packed with horses, most of them severely injured. Among them was a colt that had been trampled. The horses had been chased to exhaustion by a plane until they could be roped and dragged into the trailer she'd been following en route to be slaughtered for pet food.

Thus began a decades-long crusade against state and Federal government agencies and special interest groups to save America's wild horses. Velma Johnson's fight led her from the parched landscape of Nevada to the mountains of Montana and Wyoming and on to Washington, D.C. As a child, Velma contracted polio, but even though the disease left her somewhat crippled, it likely strengthened her resolve when fighting Washington's bureaucrats, especially those in the Bureau of Land Management, who soon nicknamed her Wild Horse Annie. In 1955, her persistence and determination led Nevada state legislators to pass a law prohibiting the use of any mechanized vehicles, including aircraft, to pursue wild horses.

What was more urgently needed, however, were Federal laws, for which she needed the confidence and help of someone in Washington. She found that person in her childhood friend Walter S. Baring, Jr., who, in 1949, had been elected to his first term in the House of Representatives. He was elected to a second two-year term, then after being defeated in 1954 was once again reelected in 1957 and served continuously until his retirement in 1973. During his tenure, Baring served as the chairman of the House Subcommittee on Public Lands, and in September, 1959, his bill that prohibited the use of mechanized vehicles in rounding up horses on any Federal land was signed into law by President Eisenhower. In her testimony before Congress to promote the bill, Velma described the cruelty of mechanized roundups and backed up her words with photographs. The bill popularly became known as the Wild Horse Annie Act.

Repeatedly in the coming years, Velma proved the public testimonies of BLM and other government officials to be not only misleading, but at times totally false. She became a key spokesperson in the fight against the BLM's efforts to eliminate the wild horse herd in Montana's Pryor Mountains, during which she was joined by Hope Ryden, then a documentary filmmaker for ABC News. Ryden's six-minute documentary, which aired during the *Evening News* on July 11, 1968, captivated millions of viewers and further weakened the BLM's position. On September 13, 1968, Secretary of Interior Stewart Udall set aside thirty-one thousand acres in the Pryor Mountains as the nation's first wild horse range.

As the public became more aware of the plight of wild horses and Velma Johnston's efforts to save them, the ranks of her supporters grew and formed organizations to help save the mustangs. At the same time, her detractors became more vocal, and thousands of wild horses continued to be rounded up illegally throughout Nevada and elsewhere and sent to California slaughterhouses. A number of gaps existed in the 1959 Wild Horse Annie Act, and by 1971, Velma was crusading for additional legislation, including a more precise definition of "a wild horse." Ranchers habitually released a handful of their branded horses into wild herds, then later rounded up all the animals, which might number two hundred or more, and sold the unbranded ones for slaughter. Even if apprehended, they used the excuse that just the opposite had occurred, that wild horses had become mixed with their horses.

Once again, Representative Walter Baring Jr. introduced just such a bill, co-sponsored in the Senate by Henry "Scoop" Jackson of Washington State and supported by many others in both chambers. By this time, even the American National Cattlemen's Association as well as the Pet Food Institute supported saving wild mustangs. Boyd Rasmussen, Director of the Bureau of Land Management, also embraced this sentiment, a dramatic reversal of the BLM's feelings a dozen years earlier.

The strongest support, however, came from school children, whom Velma had been encouraging to send letters to the congressmen. Jackson reported receiving nine thousand such letters, all in favor of saving the wild horses. In their biography, *Wild Horse Annie and the Last of the Mustangs* (2010), authors David Cruise and Alison Griffiths quote a letter from Natalie Wilkins of Jackson, Michigan that shows how the issue touched them: "Every time the men come to kill the horses for pet food I think you kill many children's hearts," she wrote. "I am a nine-year old girl and love horses. Until you do something about it you will keep many children very sad."

On December 17, 1971, President Richard Nixon signed the improved Wild Horse Annie Act into law. Officially named Public Law 92-195, or The Wild Free-Roaming Horse and Burros Act, it has been amended several times since then. While welcomed by wild horse supporters, the bill certainly has not been without controversy, as parts of the law continue to be interpreted differently by various individuals and agencies. The root of the problem is that the legislation put the Bureau of Land Management, and to a much lesser extent the U.S. Forest Service, in charge of protecting, managing, and controlling the wild herds, and the general public still does not trust them to do it.

The distrust associated with the bill stems from two sources: first, the misgivings are due largely to the fact that the BLM was not created specifically to manage wild horses; and further because of the agency's generally poor record of public relations and education programs. To legions of horse advocates, the BLM's management strategy has appeared as little more than a don't-tell-anybody-anything business in which their core mission of managing land for multiple uses simply throws wild horses into the same category as sheep, cattle, deer, and any other species on land. This is in stark contrast to the public, to whom horses, because of their intelligence, personalities, romantic history, and loyalty to their owners have always been far more personal. Indeed, some unpopular rulings by the BLM and the U.S. Forest Service have generated world-wide opposition. At the same time, the BLM feels the public does not truly understand the problems they face in trying to combine horse and land management.

"It gets emotional real quick," explained Roger Oyler, BLM Horse and Burro Specialist for the state of Arizona, during a phone conversation in mid-2016. "People either hate wild horses and burros, or they love them, and there doesn't seem to be any in-between where we can make anybody happy.

"There are far more horses and burros out there right now than the land can support. When the BLM was assigned to start managing the herds in 1971, the estimates of the total number of animals roaming the West were actually lower than what we found once we began studying the population. We often get asked why we don't just let Mother Nature manage the population naturally, but realistically that isn't an option anyone should consider," continued Oyler, who's been a horse and burro specialist with BLM for thirty years.

"Because horses do not have any real predators, they would continue to expand in numbers until they ate up their food supply, and then they'd starve. It wouldn't take long either, because a herd can double its numbers in about four years. In addition to the horses dying, they would also destroy the land, which in the dry mountain West would take decades to restore before it would support any horses again."

According to Bureau of Land Management figures, in 1971 around twenty-five thousand wild horses and burros roamed a little more than fifty-three million acres of BLM land in the ten Western states of Montana, Wyoming, Colorado, New Mexico, Arizona, Utah, Nevada, Washington, Oregon, and California. In 2015, the BLM tallied more than 58,000 horses and burros roaming the BLM's thirty-one million acres. More than twenty million acres

In 1971, when the BLM began managing the wild horse herds, there were around twenty-five thousand wild horses and burros in the West. In 2015, the number of horses and burros had grown to more than 58,000, forcing the BLM to remove many animals and offer them for adoption to the public.

has been removed or lost by the BLM through transfer to other agencies, legislation, urban expansion, court decisions, and other reasons, while the horse and burro population more than doubled.

To fulfill its obligations under the Wild Free-Roaming Horses and Burros Act, "To require the protection, management, and control of wild free-roaming horses and burros on public land," the BLM utilizes a measuring stick known as the Appropriate Management Level (AML), basically matching a herd's population with the land's capacity to support them. When the number of horses in a given location, known as a Herd Management Area, exceeds the determined management level, excess animals are removed. This is known as a "gather," and because of a little-noticed 1976 amendment to the Act, helicopters and motor vehicles may be used in these roundups. Walter Baring, Jr. had died the previous year, and while the amendment was being written into a different Congressional environmental bill, Velma herself was fighting cancer that would claim her life the following June. Thus, there was no determined opposition.

There are currently 179 Herd Management Areas across the country, and in 2015, the BLM removed a total of 3,093 horses and 726 burros in different gathers. Every animal the BLM removes is eligible for adoption by the public. The animals are kept in holding corrals, and the public is invited to view them during regularly-scheduled auctions, by visiting a holding corral, or in some cases by bidding through an internet auction. The minimum adoption fee is $125, but the bidding goes much higher for some animals. The BLM has adopted out more than 245,000 horses and burros since 1971.

"The 1971 BLM plan was originally to adopt out any excess animals we needed to remove from a management area," continued Oyler, "but we did not anticipate we would need to because the original population estimates were so low. In 2003 and 2004, we adopted out almost eight thousand horses and burros, but the number has really dropped since then and we're struggling to place as many as 2,500 animals annually now."

Animals older than ten years or those that have been passed over for adoption at least three times, can also be purchased directly from the BLM, and since 2005 more than 5,800 horses and burros have been sold to the public this way. There is a limit of four animals per person per year, to guard against buyers simply purchasing animals they intend to resell to slaughter houses.

The majority of horses purchased at a BLM auction have never seen a bridle or saddle, which means buyers must be willing to devote a lot of time to training the animal themselves. While filming wild horses in the Little Bookcliffs Wild Horse Range not far from Grand Junction, Colorado, I met John Boughton, who had adopted a BLM horse and trained it himself.

"I went over to the holding corral the day before the auction to look at the horses and connected immediately with a two-and-a-half-year-old Appaloosa mustang the BLM had originally gathered out of Wyoming at six months of age and been keeping at the Canon City facility for two years," John told me along the mountain ridge where we met. "I looked at him, and even though

John Boughton of Grand Junction, Colorado stands with the wild mustang he adopted from the BLM. He had to bid for the horse, but won with a bid of $350. He also trained the horse himself, and was able to ride the animal in less than three months.

he was in a group of horses, he raised his head and looked at me. Then, telepathically, I told him to come toward me, and he did, and on three separate occasions.

"I knew immediately he was the horse I wanted, and the bidding went up to $350 before I got him. I named him Chief Ollikut, after the brother of Chief Joseph of the Nez Perce tribe, who were known to have favored and probably helped develop Appaloosa-colored horses. That was in September, and by Thanksgiving I could saddle and ride him. Now, three years later, he's not just a horse. He's my partner. I have trained dogs for more than forty years, and the very same techniques I used for them worked on this horse, too. Time, patience, love, and understanding are the main ingredients for anyone who adopts a mustang and intends to train them. I'm convinced they're among the best horses in the country."

In an effort to increase adoptions, the BLM for years has worked closely with different prisons in which inmates train horses before the animals are put up for adoption. At every prison where such a program has been initiated, it has been extremely successful, both for the inmates as well as the horses.

"In Arizona, inmates have to apply for a training position, and then they're carefully interviewed and evaluated and have to complete their own training course," noted Oyler, describing the procedure followed at the Arizona State Prison in Florence. "The most effective trainers have no horse experience whatsoever so they're learning as they work with the animals. It takes them three to four months to get a horse trained, but when they're up for adoption, those horses typically sell for $300 to $400.

"The horse training inmates have a much lower return rate once they're released from prison," continued Oyler. "They themselves say working with horses teaches them patience, trust, and caring, usually for the first time in

Virtually every horse and burro the BLM removes from a Herd Management Area is eligible for adoption or sale. In 2003-2004, the public adopted almost eight thousand animals, but the number has since dropped considerably.

their lives, and it gives them a tremendous sense of accomplishment. Since the Florence program started in 2012, more than one hundred fifty trained horses have been adopted. In Canon City, Colorado, the inmate horse training program has been working for twenty years, so it's been a success all around."

Two additional training and adoption programs that have proven successful are those conducted by the Mustang Heritage Foundation of Georgetown, Texas. They are the Extreme Mustang Makeover and the Trainer Incentive Program (TIP), which, over the past decade, have resulted in more than five thousand wild horse adoptions from the BLM.

The Mustang Heritage Foundation's stated mission is not only to increase awareness of America's wild mustangs, but also to showcase the versatility and trainability of these horses to the public. In the Extreme Mustang Makeover competitions, which are held in nearly a dozen different cities across the United States each year, horses are carefully graded as their trainers put them through a series of difficult maneuvers and obstacles. Horses that reach the finals perform even more challenging riding tasks for which they have been trained.

What makes these events so remarkable is that the trainers themselves have to qualify in order to compete, after which they are allowed just ninety to one hundred days to choose a wild, "untouched" mustang from a BLM holding pen and completely saddle-train it. Thousands of spectators attend these Mustang Makeovers, not only to see the horses perform but also to possibly adopt one, since after each event every horse is available on a competitive bid. According to the Federation, the highest bid ever offered for a Mustang Makeover winner was $250,000.

The Foundation's Trainer Incentive Program provides opportunities to adopt a partially trained mustang at a much lower price. These horses, all three to six years old, are "gentled," which means only that they are halter broke, have been taught to load and unload from a trailer, and will allow all four hooves to be picked up for cleaning. They are available for adoption for a standard fee of just $125, the same price as an untouched horse at a BLM facility, and prospective adopters can also contract with the trainers to "finish" a horse for them if they so desire.

Not all wild horses removed from the Herd Management Areas get adopted or sold. As of 2016, more than thirteen thousand were being kept in holding corrals, and some had been held for years. Because the BLM spends roughly

Wild horses essentially have no real enemies, so herds can double their numbers in about four years. The BLM establishes the number of horses it believes the land will support, and when the number of horses exceeds that number, excess animals are removed.

two-thirds of its annual budget feeding and maintaining these animals, the agency created another program known as Off-Range Pastures, in an effort to save both the horses and their budget.

In this program, the BLM contracts with landowners to graze the horses and burros rather than raise cattle. By early 2016 almost forty-eight thousand head had been transferred to more than twenty large ranches in Kansas, Oklahoma, Montana, and other states. The average ranch size is 20,000 acres, and all the horses delivered are non-producing herds of either all mares or all geldings. The program is more cost-effective than the corrals, and at the same time allows horses to maintain free-roaming behavior for the remainder of their lives.

In 2010, the BLM started a third program, named Wild Horse EcoSanctuaries, in which herds of non-reproducing horses are contracted to private ranches with the agreement the horses must be publicly accessible with a potential for ecotourism. The funds derived from tourism are used to defray the BLM's operating payments to the land owner (in contrast to the contracted Off-Range Pastures that are not necessarily open to the public).

By mid-2016, the BLM had established three EcoSanctuaries, including Mowdy Ranch near Coalgate, Oklahoma; the Double D Ranch near Lander, Wyoming; and the original facility, the 4,700 acre Deerwood Ranch located west of Laramie, Wyoming in the beautiful Centennial Valley. I visited Deerwood on a clear but cold October morning in 2015, and came away with the belief this was a direction the BLM needed to go if it wanted to save the wild horses while at the same time educate the public.

"We were always looking for new ways to use the ranch, particularly the grass," remembered Rich Wilson as he and his wife Jana drove me around one fifteen-hundred-acre seasonal pasture that seemed filled with

In 2010, the Bureau of Land Management created Wild Horse EcoSanctuaries, the first of which was Deerwood Ranch in Centennial, Wyoming. In addition to Deerwood, the BLM now has a second EcoSanctuary near Lander, Wyoming and a third in Coalgate, Oklahoma.

In the Wild Horse EcoSanctuary program, ranch owners are required to encourage and allow visitors to see the wild horses. The herds on these ranches are non-producing, but they are allowed to basically run free on the ranches with a minimum of care.

wild horses, "and when we learned the BLM was looking for private land-owners to be part of their new EcoSanctuary program, we applied. It took almost exactly two years to get through the entire process, but because we were the pilot program, we and the BLM grew together. If we'd have a question, we'd discuss it with them, and then they'd say 'do what you think will work best, but keep us informed.' So that's what we've been doing, and after thirty years in the cattle business, it wasn't hard to become wild horse fans.

"All the horses we received were geldings, so there is no growth to the herd. The whole EcoSanctuary concept is two-fold: get the horses out of the BLM holding corrals, and to make them available for the public to see. Giving tours is one of the program's requirements, but we do it by appointment only because Jana and I also have to run the ranch itself."

Rich and Jana's first tour took place in May, 2013, when a Swiss couple drove up unannounced. They'd been to a Herd Management Area but had seen only two horses; at Deerwood, they saw three hundred wild mustangs, all at very close range. Needless to say, they were absolutely thrilled. Since then, hundreds of visitors have come to Deerwood from throughout the United States as well as from several other European countries. "Many ask if they can purchase one of the horses because they're so enthralled with the experience," added Jana, "but we're not allowed to sell any. What we do tell them is how they can participate in the BLM's adoption program, and I have to think a number of them do investigate that possibility. Others come to Deerwood with a bad opinion of the BLM, but leave with a completely different, more positive attitude, which is nice."

Rich explained how the horses are rotated through different pastures according to the season, but other than limited supplemental feeding during the

In most cases, horses that are removed range from two to about five years old. Horses older than five are more difficult for an owner to train and thus are not often adopted. Horses that are not adopted can be purchased directly from the BLM.

harsh Wyoming winter, which he and Jana choose to do, the horses are left completely alone. Some visitors ask about feeding the horses an apple or carrot, he laughed, but in actuality, these horses don't know what those treats are.

"The requirements to qualify for an EcoSanctuary are pretty extensive," noted Roger Oyler, when he and I discussed the program. "A ranch has to offer shelter, plenty of natural food, and running water, and even rocks so the horses' hooves will be worn down naturally. Really, I think it's one of our best programs, and I'm sure we'll be adding to it as much as we can."

The Pryor Mountain herd of wild horses numbers approximately one hundred fifty head, and during the summer and early autumn months, many of them graze on the high, open ridges of the Pryor Mountain Wild Horse Range, the first such designated range in the United States.

CHAPTER 8

SPECIAL HORSES IN A SPECIAL PLACE

In October, 2015, I drove to Lovell, Wyoming to study and photograph some of the most well-known wild horses in the West, the Pryor Mountain herd. They are famous for several reasons, perhaps the most important being that they are a strong example of how the local residents of Lovell and the Bureau of Land Management forged a partnership of understanding and cooperation to save the animals.

This herd, which now numbers approximately one hundred fifty head, includes a number of horses whose DNA markers match up very well with Colonial Spanish Horses, the Spanish Mustang, of the conquistadors. The lineage is not a pure one due to dilution of the bloodline by horses introduced from other areas over the years, but many animals in the herd have retained definite visible characteristics of the Spanish horses. I wanted to see those characteristics myself.

A third reason I wanted to see the Pryor Mountain horses is because they are among the most accessible of all the wild horse herds in the West. If anyone wants to see wild, free-ranging horses, and a lot of them, the chances of doing so are better here than at nearly any other place in the United States. I spotted my first horses just a few miles north of Lovell while driving up WY Highway 37, within a mile of crossing the cattle guard where I officially entered the Pryor Mountain Wild Horse Range.

This was the first Federally-established public wild horse range in the United States, created by Secretary of the Interior Stewart Udall on September 9, 1968. The boundary has been changed several times, but today the horses have approximately thirty-eight thousand acres in which to roam. It is rugged, rocky country that ranges from desert lowlands to sub-alpine meadows at an altitude of nearly nine thousand feet. Segments of the Wild Horse Range extend into the Custer National Forest and also into the Bighorn National Recreation Area.

It was just after 3 p.m., when, under a bright and warm autumn sun, I noticed a lone horse silhouetted atop a steep, rock-strewn ridge about three hundred yards away. I drove closer, then eased to the side of the road as the animal began walking along the ridge, and a few moments later it was joined by two more horses, one of them a young colt. I turned around and followed as they continued along the ridge in the direction I had just come.

I pulled ahead of the horses as the ridge dropped back down to the highway, then stood outside my vehicle as the horses passed by me at a fast trot not twenty feet away. Now there were five of them, led by a dark red bay stallion, and after crossing the highway, they continued another hundred yards straight to the shoreline of Crooked Creek Bay. It was time for their afternoon drink, followed by lazy grazing a little further down the shoreline.

The red bay stallion, I learned later when visiting the Pryor Mountain Wild Mustang Center in Lovell, was named Hickok, and his band members included Nova, a beautiful two-year-old mare; Kitalpa, a gray/black (grulla) mare born in 2010 and the mother of Nova; and Seneca, an older dun-colored mare born in 1999 and a familiar resident around Crooked Creek Bay.

The naming of the horses and compiling of their genealogy had been started decades earlier by Lynne Taylor of the Billings, Montana office of the BLM and continued by the Rev. Floyd Schwieger, a Lutheran minister in Lovell who devoted many hours to observing, studying, and photographing the horses. In 2006, Matt Dillon, the first Director of the Wild Mustang Center, began compiling the records into a database that became an important part of how the BLM currently manages the herd.

"When the BLM does a 'gather' to remove horses from the range, the Center gives them a list of specific horses, so the existing bloodline can be kept strong," Dillon told me when I contacted him by phone after I'd visited the range. "Today, only yearlings to three-year-olds are removed, because these are the most adoptable and trainable horses. The BLM doesn't remove horses every year, and when they do, the number of animals is fairly small. It's very easy for a herd of horses, here or anywhere, to multiply beyond the carrying capacity of the land, even in an area as large as this.

"The BLM posts photos of these horses on the Internet, and interested buyers submit their bids," he continued. "In 2015, the top bid for a horse was

$4,500, and the top five animals sold for an average of $2,500. The horses we have up here are in high demand, and every horse offered at auction is always sold."

The unwritten history of the Pryor Mountain wild horses dates back well over a century, and several different theories attempt to explain how the horses came to inhabit the rugged mountains straddling the Wyoming-Montana border. The mountain range itself was named after Nathaniel Pryor, a sergeant on the Lewis and Clark Expedition of 1804-06.

Assigned by Clark on July 23, 1806 to move a band of seventeen horses from their camp on the Yellowstone River over to the Missouri where Clark in-tended to use the animals to barter for trade goods with the Mandan Indians, Pryor lost the animals just two nights later to the Crow Indians. Today, the Pryor Mountain National Wild Horse Range includes a portion of the Crow Reservation, so some believe the modern herd could have started with those stolen horses.

Clark had obtained those specific horses earlier in trading with the Shoshone and Nez Perce tribes, both of whom are known to have traded for horses with Southwestern tribes like the Comanche, Apache, and Navajo, all of whom had obtained their first Spanish Colonial Horses nearly a century earlier. The Crow, like virtually all the Native American tribes, considered horses as wealth, so the only animals they would willingly have released into the Pryors would have been old, infirm horses that had little trade value, not the ones they had just stolen.

The original Spanish horses used by Cortés and the conquistadors had many different colors, one of which was gray, or *grulla*, like this mare. The narrow black stripe down its back is also common among horses with Spanish heritage.

Others believe the Pryor Mountain herd today originated some seventy-five years later, when the Crow were forced to cede part of their reservation back to the United States. Stories are told that the tribe reportedly took some of their best horses into the Pryors and secretly turned them loose, rather than handing them over to the U.S. Army. This is certainly believable, especially when, decades later in the years following World War I the Secretary of the Interior again issued an ultimatum that the Crow had to relinquish their horses and later contracted and sent special agents in to shoot the animals.

The Pryor Mountains are about seventy miles south of the Little Bighorn battlefield, and some have suggested a number of U.S. cavalry as well as Sioux and Cheyenne horses escaped the battle on June 25, 1876 and fled into the mountains to mix with tribal horses already there. What is known for certain is that the Pryor Mountains were a very important area for the Crow, as evidenced by the hundreds of tepee rings still clearly visible just west of the Wild Horse Range in an area known as Demijohn Flats. They have been carbon-dated to be at least four hundred years old.

Regardless of how the horses arrived, they survived and were present in 1894 when William and Bess Tillett homesteaded part of what is now the Wild Horse Range, south of the Custer National Forest boundary and just east of Crooked Creek. This location, combined with their love of wild horses, put the family at odds with the U.S. Forest Service and later the Bureau of Land Management for the next half century. William and Bess created the TX Ranch, encompassing some 9,000 acres and which was regularly used by the then free-roaming Pryor Mountain wild horses. Included in this herd, which eventually numbered as many as 300 animals, was a smaller herd of perhaps seventy horses that showed definite Spanish Colonial Horse characteristics.

Off and on through the years, the Forest Service attempted to remove the horses, or to confine them by fencing in portions of national forest, but their efforts were largely unsuccessful. Forest Ranger Charles O. Williamson resigned because he refused to remove any of the Spanish horses, as ordered to by his superiors. The U.S. Grazing Service, later enlarged to become the Bureau of Land Management, issued grazing permits and established allotment boundaries, including twenty horse permits to the Tilletts, who were later cited by the BLM because far more than twenty horses were "trespassing" on their allotment.

According to researcher and author Christine Reed, who has spent years studying the history of the Pryor Mountain horses and whose detailed work, *Saving the Pryor Mountain Mustang* (2015), documents the efforts to either

The Pryor Mountain Wild Horse Range embraces thirty-eight thousand acres, and includes desert grassland as well as sub-alpine meadows at an elevation of nearly nine thousand feet. Portions of the Wild Horse Range extend into both the Custer National Forest as well as the Bighorn National Recreation Area.

remove or protect them, the Tillett-BLM feud boiled over in 1966 when the BLM suspended the Tilletts' horse and cattle permits because of their refusal to remove the trespassing horses. To protect the horses from BLM removal, Lloyd Tillett, William's son, then stepped in to claim ownership of the animals.

This long, continuous controversy had not gone unnoticed by the citizens of Lovell, many of whom sided with the Tilletts in believing the wild horses had an historical right to remain wild and free in the Pryors. On April 8, 1966, a group of these advocates met with BLM officials and the Tillett family to try to settle the dispute. By meeting's end, the Tilletts had agreed to give up their claim to the wild horses on their allotment, and in return, the BLM restored the Tillett's grazing permits. Just as importantly, the BLM agreed to conduct a detailed study of range conditions in the area, and until this study was completed, the horses would be left undisturbed.

Although this meeting did not resolve all the issues permanently, it set the stage for far-reaching future and historical impacts not only on the Pryor Mountain herd, but also on wild horse herds throughout the West. For the first time, a wild horse herd was officially recognized as part of America's western heritage.

As the BLM grazing study continued, Lovell residents began laying plans for a wild horse visitor center, and asked both the BLM and National Park Service to create an easily accessible wild horse range where the public could view the horses. Lovell's concession was to agree to have the herd reduced to about one hundred horses. There were additional setbacks, however, as the BLM found itself in the middle of a problem it couldn't solve on its own: set aside land for wild horses while at the same time manage that land for other local uses, such as cattle ranching or big game hunting.

A number of horses in the Pryor Mountain herd exhibit Spanish markings, such as this animal that has dark "zebra stripes" on its front legs. This particular horse also has a dark stripe down its back, although it doesn't show in this photograph.

They proposed different options, including one that would reduce the herd to less than two dozen head. Even with that small number, the citizens of Lovell would have to be totally responsible for them, as well as keep the herd at that number. Obviously, this proposal was not a satisfactory one and the impasse continued.

As publicity increased, the Pryor Mountain wild horse issue spread well beyond Lovell, and before long included state senators Mike Mansfield of Montana and Clifford Hansen of Wyoming; Hope Ryden, a feature producer for ABC Evening News; and nationally-known wild horse advocate Velma B. "Wild Horse Annie" Johnson. Hundreds of others nationwide wrote letters, signed petitions, and even telegrammed the Lovell Chamber of Commerce, all in favor of saving the horses. Finally, on September 9, 1968, bowing to intense political pressure, Secretary of the Interior Stuart Udall designated thirty-one thousand acres in the Pryor Mountains as the Pryor Mountain Wild Horse Range.

Under Udall's directive, the BLM was charged with the responsibility of developing a wild horse management plan for the area, and not surprisingly, Lovell's Pryor Mountain Wild Mustang Association, which had kept the preservation battle going, was the first to offer its assistance to the BLM, and the BLM accepted their help. One of the major areas of cooperation between the two groups was the BLM's acceptance of the Association's years of record keeping that indicated the Pryor Mountain herd did, in fact, include many animals showing body conformation and coloration indicative of Colonial Spanish Horse descent. Both parties agreed these were the horses that needed to be preserved.

"As a result of this trust between the BLM and the citizens of Lovell, the management of the Pryor Mountain herd not only got started in the right direction, but has, for the most part, been continuing in the right direction for more than four decades," Dillon told me in early 2016. "Neither group could have successfully managed these horses alone for such a long time, but together using each other's knowledge and resources, we've been able to do it very successfully, and it was a pleasure working with the BLM, particularly their wild horse and burro specialist, Jared Bybee."

After several days of observing and photographing the horses along Hwy. 37, I joined two other visitors on a guided tour with Steve Cerroni, a Lovell resident who takes visitors into the Pryors to see the wild horses. A Wisconsin native, Cerroni bought his first horse at age thirteen because all he ever wanted to be was a cowboy. He moved to Montana in 1989 to follow that dream, going to work on a guest ranch just north of the Pryor Mountains. Part of his job was to meet ranch guests at the airport in Billings and bring them to the ranch, and in so doing they drove through the Wild Horse Range.

"It seemed like every guest always wanted to see the mustangs," Cerroni remembered as he slowly negotiated his Jeep up a steep, rocky path named Burnt Timber Road that led to the summit ridge of the Pryor Range twelve miles away. "I realized there was a tremendous interest in the horses because whenever we'd see them, I'd have to stop and let the guests photograph them. The comment I heard most often was simply 'Unbelievable'."

Cerroni, now over sixty years old, began leading tours for the Pryor Mountain Wild Mustang Center in Lovell in 2014, and that first year he had visitors from nearly every state as well as from nine foreign countries. In 2015 the number of tours he led tripled, and that winter the Mustang Center bought a second vehicle in order to be able to meet the growing demand for wild horse viewing. The trips last a full day, include a sandwich lunch, and cost $200 per person.

Not long after topping out on the ridge—we weren't completely above treeline, but the terrain now included hundreds of acres of rich, rolling grassland—we saw our first group of horses, a band of six or seven that crossed in front of us from right to left. They weren't running fast, but they did not stop

Like all wild horse herds, the animals are grouped together in bands of several mares and their foals that are controlled by a single stallion. Here a band gathers at a small pond for an afternoon drink.

The mares foal through the spring and into the summer. Here a very young foal stays by its mother's side as they feed together.

to look at us out of curiosity. Turning the Jeep to follow them, Cerroni topped a low rise and there before us grazed as many as eighty or ninety horses. It reminded me of an experience I'd had years before in the Serengeti of Tanzania, in which my guide and I had driven for more than an hour without observing a single animal. Then we topped a hill to suddenly see the entire world filled with migrating wildebeest. Like those wildebeest, even though the horses could clearly see and hear us, they were totally unconcerned at our presence.

One dun-colored stallion stood near the Jeep road guarding his band of mares that were resting beneath a grove of nearby spruce trees, and because the stallion had very clear Colonial Spanish markings, including zebra stripes on both front legs and a dark dorsal stripe, I stepped out to study and photograph the horse more closely. In his "North American Colonial Spanish Horse Update" of July 2011, Dr. Phil Sponenberg, DVM, PhD at Virginia Tech University in Blacksburg, described the Pryor Mountain mustangs as "an important resource for Spanish Horse conservation," and added that "not only do many of these horses have Spanish conformation but that the blood types of the horses are also those expected of horses with Spanish ancestry."

This was exactly the type of horse I'd come to see, and the primitive markings are known as the Dun factor. Not all the horses in this herd have these markings, and as I slowly circled to get different photography angles, I was surprised to see how calm the horse remained. Cerroni had told me the Pryor horses are generally unafraid of people and that as long as I moved slowly and quietly, I'd be able to get all the photos I wanted, and he was right.

As we walked among the horses, Cerroni identified them by name. Each year, he and his wife Nancy publish the *Field Guide to the Pryor Mountain Wild Horses*, for which he takes many of the photographs. Because they have both spent so much time studying the animals, they not only know all of them by name but also their backgrounds. This is the information the BLM depends on when they're removing specific horses for auction.

Although nearly a hundred horses contentedly grazed around us, they were actually separated into different bands of mares, each controlled by a single stallion. Other stallions, especially younger ones, would occasionally try to lure or steal a mare from one of the bands, and while we witnessed no actual fighting, several times we did see an older stallion driving one of the younger ones away.

Later we walked across a meadow to a small rise where we could look down to a natural pond

The Pryor Mountain wild horses have inhabited this rugged region on the Wyoming/Montana border for well over a century, and because of their Spanish markings, are highly sought by individuals when excess animals are offered for adoption.

and watched two different bands of horses come down to drink. Cerroni was searching for a particular stallion, a pale-colored palomino roan named Cloud that is quite possibly the most famous wild horse in America today, and certainly the best known of the Pryor Mountain horses.

Cloud's story began in 2001 with the airing of a PBS *Nature* series program named "Cloud: Wild Stallion of the Rockies," a film produced by Ginger Kathrens, who at the time worked for Marty Stouffer, host of the PBS series *Wild America*. The initial film was extremely popular, and there is no question Kathrens helped alert the world to the existence of wild horses in the West, and to the Pryor Mountain herd in particular.

Two years later, she followed with "Cloud's Legacy: The Wild Stallion Returns," and in 2009 she added "Cloud: Challenge of the Stallions." Like her first film, these were also popular with the public and helped make both young and old alike aware of the problems and difficulties facing wild horses today. She has continued these efforts through additional films, books, and other educational programs as the founder and chairman of The Cloud Foundation in Colorado Springs.

Cloud was born in the Pryor Mountains in 1995 to a black stallion named Raven and a bright palomino mare named Phoenix, and over the past two decades he has not only been a beautiful but also a dominant herd stallion, producing numerous offspring. The problem is that Cloud's grandfather, a buckskin, was one of several animals introduced into the Pryor Mountains from a different BLM herd management area in Rock Springs, Wyoming in the 1980s to add genetic diversity. Neither Cloud's grandfather, nor his father Raven, nor Cloud himself has a definitive Spanish Colonial Horse background.

In essence, the most famous wild horse in the Pryor Mountain herd and his ancestors diluted the ancient Spanish bloodline for years. When I asked Dr. Phil Sponenberg about this in January 2016, his e-mail reply was very revealing. "The Pryor horses are no longer all that important for conserving Colonial Spanish-type," he wrote me. "The color on the duns/grullos is a trivial aspect, and doesn't really connect much to its uniquely Spanish origin.

"I do not envy the BLM managers their task, because Cloud and his family are the source of the non-Spanish influence, and are so very popular with the public."

Both the Pryor Mountain Mustang Center and the BLM have, through the years, identified and removed many of Cloud's offspring and auctioned them to the public, in efforts to maintain as much purity in the Spanish bloodline as possible. By the spring of 2016, Cloud himself, then twenty-one years old, had become a bachelor stallion without his own band of mares so his influence was also in decline. Long before Cloud's dominance began, however, the Pryor horses had survived genetic dilution from numerous other sources.

This included from horses brought in by early homesteaders. The Tilletts were only one of many families who claimed land in the area in the 1890s. In addition, horses from later ranches probably found their way into the herd in the decades following the homesteaders. Nonetheless, many Pryor horses today still retain the smaller stature, dun coloration, and leg and back markings characteristic of a Colonial Spanish heritage, reason enough to work for their continued preservation.

As we climbed into Cerroni's Jeep for the trip down the mountain and return to Lovell, he turned on the CD player, and chose a particular song for us. Its title was "La Primera," written and recorded by legendary Canadian singer Ian Tyson. The song, a beautiful, haunting ballad included in Tyson's album *Lost Herd*, accurately describes the history of America's Spanish Mustangs, from the time of Columbus' arrival in 1493 to the present day horses Cerroni and I had spent the day observing in the Pryor Mountains. Tyson mentions the Pryor Mountain horses in the song, and after returning home, I telephoned Ian at his ranch in Alberta to talk about "La Primera."

"My whole life has been centered around horses," he told me. "I started as a rodeo rider when I was still a teenager, and now here on my ranch I still have five horses, and I've had all of them a long time. The funny thing is, I didn't get into the music business until I was recovering from a rodeo injury. I've traveled all over the world, but at the same time, I've never been far from horses."

In the early 1960s, Tyson was half of the well-known folk singing duo Ian and Sylvia, and his song "Four Strong Winds" is considered a folk classic. In 1979, he retired briefly to work on his 500-acre ranch, and by the time he returned to music just a few years later, the folk era had ended. He began to write and record cowboy songs. "La Primera," popular with wild horse lovers everywhere, was released in 1999.

"Wild horses are a fascinating subject to me," continued Ian, eighty-two at the time of our conversation, "and I did a lot of reading and research on the horses before I actually wrote 'La Primera'." The first book I read was Frank Dobie's *The Mustangs* (1952), but I read a lot of other books, too. It wasn't my easiest song to write, because I wanted to tell their entire history in America. I had known about the Pryor horses for years and included them, but I didn't actually get to see them personally until 2007. I spent a day up in those high meadows just looking at them.

"One of the colors they often talk about in Spanish horses is dun, or a type of light brown, but sometimes darker hairs can be mixed with the brown, and this is called coyote dun, and I used this in 'La Primera.' When you go up into the Pryors, you'll see that exact color, too."

Well-known recording artist Ian Tyson's song "La Primera" continues to be popular today, more than a decade after its release. Tyson spent a lot of time studying the history of wild horses before writing the lyrics, and later visited the Pryor Mountain Wild Horse Range. Photo Credit: Ian Tyson/Slick Fork Music.

"La Primera"

Written by Ian Tyson, Slick Fork Music (reprinted with permission)

It was a long hard voyage to the Americas in 1493
I was afraid that I would die of thirst.
The little mare beside me died
and was put into the sea, but I survived.
I swam to shore, I am La Primera.

When Cortés sailed for Mexico
From that island in the sun
There were sixteen of us sorrels, blacks and bays.
One of them was my first born,
He was called the Coyote Dun.
He survived and conquered all of Mexico.

I am a drinker of the wind.
I am the one who never tires.
I love my freedom more than all these things.
The conquistador, Comanche and the cowboy
I carried them to glory.
I am La Primera– Spanish Mustang,
Hear my story.

Those Comanches were holy terrors
When they climbed up on backs.
When the grass was high
They would raid for a thousand miles.
But the Texans had revolvers
When they came back from the war.
The buffalo had gone
The Comanche moon was waning.

So it's come along boys and listen to my tale,
We are following the longhorn cow,
Going up Mister Goodnight's trail you see.
Those cowboys were kind to us,
We listened to their sad songs
All the way to the far Saskatchewan.

High in the Pryor Mountains
First light of Dawn,
Coyote Dun walks beneath the morning star.
He became an outlaw, his blood was watered some,
But the flame still burns
Into the new millennium.

I am a drinker of the wind.
I am the one who never tires.
I love my freedom more than all these things.
The conquistador, Comanche and the cowboy
I carried them to glory.
I am La Primera—Spanish Mustang,
La Primer—Spanish Mustang.

APPENDIX

Public Law 92-195

The Wild Free-Roaming Horses And Burros Act
December 15, 1971

An Act

To require the protection, management, and control of wild free-roaming horses and burros on public lands.

Be it enacted by the Senate and House of Representatives of the United States of America in Congress assembled. That Congress finds and declares that wild free-roaming horses and burros are living symbols of the historic and pioneer spirit of the West; that they contribute to the diversity of life forms within the Nation and enrich the lives of the American people; and that these horses and burros are fast disappearing from the American scene. It is the policy of Congress that wild free-roaming horses and burros shall be protected from capture, branding, harassment, or death; and to accomplish this they are to be considered in the area where presently found, as an integral part of the natural system of the public lands.

Sec. 2. As used in this act–

(a) "Secretary" means the Secretary of the Interior when used in connection with public land administered by him through the Bureau of Land Management and the Secretary of Agriculture in connection with public lands administered by him through the Forest Service;

(b) "wild free-roaming horses and burros" means all unbranded and unclaimed horses and burros on public lands of the United States;

(c) "range" means the amount of land necessary to sustain an existing herd or herds of wild free-roaming horses and burros, which does not exceed their known territorial limits, and which is devoted principally but not necessarily exclusively to their welfare in keeping with the multiple-use management concept for the public lands;

(d) "herd" means one or more stallions and his mares; and

(e) "public lands" means any lands administered by the Secretary of the Interior through the Bureau of Land Management or by the Secretary of Agriculture through the Forest Service.

Sec. 3

(a) All wild free-roaming horses and burros are hereby declared to be under the jurisdiction of the Secretary for the purpose of management and protection in accordance with the provisions of this Act. The Secretary is authorized and directed to protect and manage wild free-roaming horses and burros as components of the public lands, and he may designate and maintain specific ranges on public lands as sanctuaries for their protection and preservation, where the Secretary after consultation with the wildlife agency of the State Board established in section 7 of this Act deems such action desirable. The Secretary shall manage wild free-roaming horses and burros in a manner that is designed to achieve and maintain a thriving ecological balance on the public lands. He shall consider the recommendations of qualified scientists in the field of biology and ecology, some of whom shall be independent of both Federal and State agencies and may include members of the Advisory Board established in section 7 of this Act. All management activities shall be at the minimal feasible level and shall be carried out in consultation with the wildlife agency of the State wherein such lands are located in order to protect the natural ecological balance of all wildlife species which inhabit such lands, particularly endangered wildlife species. Any adjustments in forage allocations on any such lands shall take into consideration the needs of other wildlife species which inhabit such lands.

(b) Where an area is found to be overpopulated, the Secretary, after consulting with the Advisory Board, may order old, sick, or lame animals to be destroyed in the most humane manner possible, and he may cause additional excess wild free-roaming horses and burros to be captured and removed for private maintenance under humane conditions and care.

(c) The Secretary may order wild free-roaming horses and burros to be destroyed in the most humane manner possible when he deems such action to be an act of mercy or when his judgment such action is necessary to preserve and maintain the habitat in a suitable condition for continued use. No wild free-roaming horse or burro shall be ordered to be destroyed because of overpopulation unless in the judgment of the Secretary such action is the only practical way to remove excess animals from the area.

(d) Norhing in this Act shall preclude the customary disposal of the remains of a deceased wild free-roaming horse or burro, including those in the authorized possession of private parties, but in no event shall such remains, or any part thereof, be sold for any consideration, directly or indirectly.

Sec. 4. If wild free-roaming horses or burros stray from public lands onto privately owned land, the owners of such land may inform the nearest Federal marshal or agent of the Secretary, who shall arrange to have the animals removed. In no event shall such wild free-roaming horses and burros be destroyed except by the agents of the Secretary. Nothing in this section shall be construed to prohibit a private landowner from maintaining wild free-roaming horses or burros on his private lands, or lands leased from the Government, if he does so in a matter that protects them from harassment, and if the animals were not willfully removed or enticed from the public lands. Any individuals who maintain such wild free-roaming horses or burros on their private lands or lands leased from the Government shall notify the appropriate agent of the Secretary and supply him with a reasonable approximation of the number of animals so maintained.

Sec. 5. A person claiming ownership of a horse or burro on the public lands shall be entitled to recover it only if recovery is permissible under the branding and estray laws of the State in which the animal is found.

Sec. 6. The Secretary is authorized to enter into cooperative agreements with other landowners and with the State and local governmental agencies and may issue such regulations as he deems necessary for the furtherance of the purposes of this Act.

Sec. 7. The Secretary of the Interior and the Secretary of Agriculture are authorized and directed to appoint a joint advisory board of not more than nine members to advise them on any matter relating to wild free-roaming horses and burros and their management and protection. They shall select as advisors persons who are not employees of the Federal or State Governments, and whom they deem to have special knowledge about protection of horses and burros, management of wildlife, animal husbandry, or natural resources

management. Members of the board shall not receive reimbursement except for travel and other expenditures necessary in connection with their services.
  Sec. 8

(a) Any person who –
  (1) willfully removes or attempts to remove a wild free-roaming horse or burro from the public lands, without authority from the Secretary, or
  (2) converts a wild free-roaming horse or burro to private use, without authority from the Secretary, or
  (3) maliciously causes the death or harassment of any wild free-roaming horse or burro, or
  (4) processes or permits to be processed into commercial products the remains of a wild free-roaming horse or burro, or
  (5) willfully violates a regulation issued pursuant to this Act, shall be subject to a fine of not more than $2,000, or imprisonment for not more than one year, or both. Any person so charged with such violation by the Secretary may be tried and sentenced by any United States commissioner or magistrate designated for that purpose by the court by which he was appointed, in the same manner and subject to the same conditions as provided for in section 3401, title 18, United States Code.
(b) Any employee designated by the Secretary of the Interior or the Secretary of Agriculture shall have power, without warrant, to arrest any person committing in the presence of such an employee a violation of this Act or any regulation made pursuant thereto, and to take such person immediately for examination or trial before an officer or court of competent jurisdiction, and shall have power to execute any warrant or other process issued by an officer or court of competent jurisdiction to enforce the provisions of this Act or regulations made pursuant thereto. Any judge of a court established under the laws of the United States, or any United States magistrate may, within his respective jurisdiction, upon proper oath or affirmation showing probably cause, issue warrants in all such cases.

  Sec. 9. Nothing in this Act shall be construed to authorize the Secretary to relocate wild free-roaming horses or burros to areas of the public lands where they do not presently exist.
  Sec. 10. After the expiration of thirty calendar months following the date enactment of this Act, and every twenty-four calendar months thereafter, the Secretaries of the Interior and Agriculture shall submit to Congress a joint

report on the administration of this Act, including a summary of enforcement and /or other actions taken thereunder, costs, and such recommendations for legislative or other actions as he might deem appropriate.

The Secretary of the Interior and the Secretary of Agriculture shall consult with respect to the implementation and enforcement of this Act and to the maximum feasible extent coordinate the activities of their respective departments and in the implementation and enforcement of this Act.

The Secretaries are authorized and directed to undertake those studies of the habits of wild free-roaming horses and burros that they may deem necessary in order to carry out the provisions of this Act.

ACKNOWLEDGMENTS

America's wild horses, especially those we describe as Spanish Mustangs, are both historic and iconic animals, and as such they have been studied and written about by scholars for years. Writers of history often find themselves referring to many of the same sources as previous writers, but I am particularly indebted to two historians in New Mexico whose earlier works proved to be extremely important throughout my own research. They are William W. Dunmire and Marc Simmons, neither of whom needs any introduction to students of Southwestern history. I referred to their works frequently, either to guide me in a certain direction, or to confirm a fact I had found elsewhere.

Another author whose work I found particularly helpful and who deserves a special mention includes Dr. Jay F. Kirkpatrick, who was both a pioneer as well as a strong advocate of artificial population management techniques among wild horse herds. Unfortunately, Dr. Kirkpatrick died unexpectedly in December 2015 before I had a chance to visit with him but he was known and highly thought of by many I met later.

I have not met author J. Edward de Steiguer, but his book, *Wild Horses of the West* (2011), filled in a number of gaps for me along the way. His scholarly research is remarkable and anyone interested in wild horses will gain added insight by reading his book.

In my travels around the West in studying wild horses, a number of individuals graciously donated their time to help me get the photographs or the information I needed. Among them are Steve Cerroni, who provided an unforgettable day with the Pryor Mountain horses high in Wyoming and Montana; Rich and Jana Wilson, owners of the Deerwood Ranch Wild Horse EcoSanctuary near Centennial, Wyoming; and Sean Kelly of the Jicarilla

Ranger District in the Carson National Forest, who pinpointed several locations where I was able to film my first wild horses for this book.

Later, at Bent's Old Fort in Colorado, John Carson, great-grandson of mountain man and explorer Kit Carson, spent a full day with me, talking about wild horses and describing how they and the fort played such an important role in the opening of the West. Joining John in our discussions were two other historians, Jim Sebastian and Sam Pisciotta, both of whom were more than gracious in sharing their own research with me. Aaron Roth, Historic Site Manager at the Bosque Redondo Memorial at Fort Sumner, added to John's information and provided valuable access to old archives that included Carson's own correspondence.

Donna Mitchell, co-founder of the Spanish Mustang Foundation, drove me through a morning snow shower to show me the Spanish Mustangs on her ranch near Cerrillos, New Mexico, then followed up with a cup of steaming coffee as she and her husband Jim entertained me with more stories of training and working with wild mustangs through the years. Along a dusty trail in Colorado, John Boughton not only described to me how he adopted a wild mustang, he unloaded the horse from his trailer just so I could get a good look at the animal.

I am also indebted to Roger Oyler, Horse and Burro Specialist for the Bureau of Land Management for the state of Arizona, who visited with me by phone for much of one morning in July, 2016. Roger postponed his paperwork and other phone calls to educate me about the Bureau's wild horse management programs, and his experience both in the field and in dealing with writers like myself was clearly evident. I owe him a huge vote of appreciation. Two others who returned my phone calls and e-mails and helped immensely with my research were two of America's foremost geneticists who have studied Spanish Colonial Horses for many years, Dr. Gus Cothran of Texas A&M University; and Dr. Phil Sponenberg of Virginia Tech University.

When I telephoned recording artist Ian Tyson at his ranch in Alberta, I felt as if I were talking to an old friend, as I've been listening to his music for decades. Ian has actually enjoyed two singing careers, the first in folk music and the second in Western "cowboy" songs, as he describes them. He was as gracious on the telephone as he is on stage, and his wild mustang song, "La Primera," continues to be a favorite among horse lovers throughout the West.

Finally, I want to thank my long-time friend and mentor, Don Lambert of Airbrush Imaging in Weatherford, Texas. As he has done a number of times over the years, Don willingly shared his computer and Photoshop expertise with me to improve or even save a number of images that appear in this book.

BIBLIOGRAPHY

Ambrose, Stephen E. *Undaunted Courage*. New York: Simon & Schuster, 1996.

Bennett, Deb, PhD. *Conquerors*. Solvang, CA: Amigo Publications, 1998.

Brislawn, Mabel. *Spanish Mustangs and Hard Times*. Oshoto, WY: Bob Brislawn Society, 2014.

Clark, Ella E. *Indian Legends from the Northern Rockies*. Norman: Univ. of Oklahoma Press, 1966.

Connell, Evan S. *Son of the Morning Star*. New York: Farrar, Straus and Giroux, 1984.

Crow, Joseph Medicine. *From the Heart of Crow Country*. New York: Orion Books, 1992.

_____.*Counting Coup*. Washington, DC: National Geographic Society, 2006.

Cruise, David and Griffiths, Alison. *Wild Horse Annie*. New York: Scribner, 2010.

Dary, David. *The Santa Fe Trail*. New York: Alfred A. Knopf, 2000.

De Steiguer, J. Edward. *Wild Horses of the West*. Tucson: Univ. of Arizona Press, 2011.

Dobie, J. Frank. *The Mustangs*. Edison, NJ: Castle Books, 1934.

Dunmire, William W. *New Mexico's Spanish Livestock Heritage*. Albuquerque: Univ. of New Mexico Press, 2013.

Favour, Alpheus H. *Old Bill Williams, Mountain Man.* Norman: Univ. of Oklahoma Press, 1962.

Graham, Don. *Kings of Texas.* Hoboken, NJ: John Wiley & Sons, 2003.

Gregg, Josiah. *Commerce of the Prairies.* Norman: Univ. of Oklahoma Press, 1954.

Gwynne, S. C. *Empire of the Summer Moon.* New York: Scribner, 2010.

Hunter, J. Marvin (Editor). *The Trail Drivers of Texas.* Nashville: Cokesbury Press, 1925.

Johnson, Gary, Fischer, James, and Geer, Harold. *Custer's Horses.* Prescott, AZ: Wolfe Publishing, 2000.

Kirkpatrick, Jay F. *Into the Wind.* Minocqua, WI: NorthWord Press, 1994.

Lavender, David. *Bent's Fort.* New York: Doubleday & Co., 1954.

Lawrence, Elizabeth Atwood. *Comanche.* Detroit: Wayne State University Press, 1989.

Lockwood, Frank C. *The Apache Indians.* Lincoln: Univ. of Nebraska Press, 1938.

Morgan, Phyllis S. *As Far As the Eye Could Reach.* Norman: Univ. of Oklahoma Press, 2015.

Morin, Paula. *Honest Horses.* Reno, NV: University of Nevada Press, 2006.

Preston, Douglas. *Cities of Gold.* New York: Simon & Schuster, 1992.

Reed, Christine. *Saving the Pryor Mountain Mustang.* Reno, NV: Univ. of Nevada Press, 2015.

Roberts, David. *The Pueblo Revolt.* New York: Simon & Schuster, 2004.

_____.*A Newer World.* New York: Simon & Schuster, 2000.

Rojas, Arnold R. *These Were The Vaqueros.* Santa Ynez, CA: Alamar Media, 2010.

Ryden, Hope. *America's Last Wild Horses.* New York: E.P. Dutton & Co., 1970.

Simmons, Marc. The Last Conquistador. Norman: Univ. of Oklahoma Press, 1991.

_____.*Spanish Pathways*. Albuquerque: Univ. of New Mexico Press, 2001.

Stands In Timber, John. *Cheyenne Memories*. Lincoln: Bison Books, 1967.

Underhill, Ruth M. *The Navajos*. Norman: University of Oklahoma Press, 1956.

Wallace, Ernest and Hoebel, E. Adamson. *The Comanches*. Norman: Univ. of Oklahoma Press, 1952.

Weber, David J. *The Taos Trappers*. Norman: Univ. of Oklahoma Press, 1971.

ABOUT THE AUTHOR

Steve Price has been a fulltime writer and photographer for more than forty years, specializing in outdoor recreation, nature photography, and travel. He has written more than three thousand magazine articles for dozens of publications, and fifteen books ranging from fishing to African wildlife. One of his earlier books, *Valley of the Big Cats*, received international acclaim, and his photography has won national and international awards. He has traveled widely throughout the world, and currently serves as a Contributing Editor for *Field & Stream* and as a columnist for the Yamaha Marine Group. A native of Texas and a former resident of northwestern Wyoming, he lives in Tijeras, New Mexico, where he rides horses several times a week.

INDEX